the
NOTEBOOK
MEETING

How to Finally Organize
Your Life and Reach
Your Mountaintop Moments

STUART ANDERSON

The notebook-meeting process can
help you find the meaning, fulfillment,
and success in life that is yours to claim.

ISBN: 0-692-84668-9
ISBN-13: 978-0-692-84668-1
Library of Congress Cataloging-In-Publication Data
A catalog record for this book is available from the Library of Congress

Cover Photography by Morgan Corbett Photography
www.morgancorbett.com
Cover and Interior Design by Tara Mayberry, TeaBerryCreative.com
Styling by Saltbox Lane
www.instagram.com/saltboxlane/

*Dedicated to all who choose
to start their own notebook meetings—
the world needs your work.*

CONTENTS

Morning Light

Lyrics by Josh Garrels
REPRINTED WITH PERMISSION

There's a place, a garden for the young
To laugh and dance in safety among
The shimmering light in the garden of peace

But steal a bite and paradise is lost
With darkened hearts we didn't count the cost
Forgot all we left behind

Life picks up speed before you know
We hold on for dear life, Oh Lord
We're too proud to turn back now

One day it all falls down
It breaks our heart and it breaks our crown
Brings us down where we see

It's gonna be all right
Turn around and let back in the light
And joy will come
Like a bird in the morning sun
And all will be made well
Once again

There's a way that seems right to a man
Until he's in over head and he don't understand
How the plans he made only led him astray

But every good gift comes down from above
From the Lord of light like a labor of love
Upon the child who waits for Him

Sometimes you'll find what you're waiting for
Was there all along just waiting for you
To turn around and reconcile
And it may be broken down
All the bridges burned like an old ghost town
But this my son can be made new

It's gonna be all right
Shake it out and let back in the light
And joy will come
Like a bird in the morning sun
And all will be made well
And all will be made well
And all will be made well
Once again

From Josh Garrel's album Home
Released April 7, 2015

INTRODUCTION

For all of us, whether we are a family of one or a family of ten, the day-to-day life events we face are the greatest threats to our happiness, success, and most importantly, our ability to love one another... especially those we call our own. Our days are filled with the busyness of managing lives. Too often we lay our heads on our pillows at night wondering where the time went—another day spent on activities that don't match the desires of our hearts. If you desire to become more intentional and purposeful about really living your life, it is time to schedule your first notebook meeting.

STUART

That is my name; I am female. I am a wife, mother, business partner, educator, consultant, and writer. I have a passion for helping families and individuals go forward toward the greater good. As I write this, I have lived the "notebook meeting" for about twelve years. Life revealed the process to me in pieces as I lived through the struggles, challenges, mistakes, revelations, blessings, and successes we all encounter in daily life. I was stuck in my own clutter and chaos before the notebook-meeting process became clear. *I am you*, except that I have a twelve-year head start on using the notebook meetings.

Writing the notebook meeting down in a format that you can use is one of my life's works. I know it will help you find your greater good. I cannot wait for you to get started.

DAVID

David is my husband and one of the wisest and most loving men I know. You will read his name in this book. He is a father, psychotherapist, professional speaker, and writer. He has been a tremendous part of the notebook-meeting process and is responsible for some of the material in this book. He is delighted that I am using his material. I am delighted to be married to David. Our marriage is strengthened when we have notebook meetings. You can connect with David at **www.impactingpeople.com**.

EMOTIONAL CONTENT

You will react in a multitude of ways to various parts of this book. Sometimes you might smile in acknowledgment, grunt in resistance, or wrinkle your face in confusion. I am writing about a journey that will change your life, so it will be an emotional experience.

What will you do when I mention God? He is part of my journey. His name appears when I share excerpts from my notebook meetings. Knowing about God is not a requirement of the notebook-meeting process. It is my belief that this book would not exist without Him. I also believe He will help you reach your mountaintop moments if you let Him. You do not have to believe what I believe. But...if you ever want to hear more about Him, I would love to share.

PRINCIPLES OF
THE NOTEBOOK-MEETING
PROCESS

1. You *will* organize your life, and this time it *will* stick.
2. You *will* accomplish goals that have previously seemed unreachable.
3. It is an ongoing process that *will* change your life. You *will* never want it to end.
4. You are not perfect, and neither am I. We can forgive ourselves for all the times we did not get it right. This time we *will*.
5. No one else can do the work for you. You have to do the work. You *will* be able to figure it out.

Will it so, my friend; will it so.

SUGGESTIONS FOR HOW TO READ THIS BOOK

First of all, let me tell you that *The Notebook Meeting* is for *anyone*. Whether you are female or male, married or single, employed or not, *The Notebook Meeting* can change your life for the better. I know this without a doubt. The process, as I write it in the following chapters, is really about a lifestyle that will help you become organized, balanced, and proactive as you manage the events of day-to-day living. The notebook-meeting process will also show you how to do the work to accomplish every one of your dreams and goals, or what I call your *mountaintop moments*.

This is definitely a "work" book. There are actions for you to complete throughout the chapters. I suggest you read the chapters in order and complete the actions as they are written. As soon as you complete one action, take time to reflect if needed. Then keep going to the next step. Do not let too much time lapse between chapters, or you will forget important steps in the process. My heart's desire is that you will realize more than ever before that your dreams and goals are closer to being your reality. I truly want that for you.

I must also admit that I have a larger agenda in mind. I believe that when *you* change your life for the better, it affects the lives of all of us for the better. If we all work to change our lives for the better, we will affect our neighborhoods, schools, churches, workplaces, communities, and *our world*.

Let's get started.

NOTE TO READERS

We have to include some legal talk. This book contains the opinions and ideas of the author. The stylistic choices and grammatical mistakes are hers. This book is intended to help you change your life for the better, but the author is not rendering professional advice. Of course, the strategies might not work for everyone. Thus, any results cannot be guaranteed. As noted in the book, you may need to consult a professional before you implement the strategies. The author welcomes your constructive comments. You may find her contact information at **www.thenotebookmeeting.com**.

Bless you on your journey.

CHAPTER ONE

IN THE BEGINNING

*Flickers of light, hope, and possibility
are about to shine in your life.*

Organizing Your Life

Hmmm, organizing your life.

Take a moment to think about that. What does your mind begin to visualize? What exactly do you see? An orderly house; closets with clothes arranged for the season, shoes and purses fitting perfectly on shelves; food for dinner prepared in the fridge; laundry all folded and put away; and kids' toys corralled in tubs? Or, as you think about the organized life, perhaps you see yourself celebrating the early completion of a big project at work with dinner out (on a weeknight, no less) with your husband. Maybe in the organized life, you see yourself with time to spend in your craft room or garden after a full day of work or simply sitting with a cup of hot tea and your favorite magazine. Maybe your husband is sitting right beside you reading as well, and the kids are quietly finishing their homework at the kitchen table before you all gather for dinner. Your vision of the organized life is full of images

1

that bring you peace and also some confident hope that tomorrow will be somewhat of a repeat of the picture just described, right?

So, let me ask you this question: Do you feel that way generally— a little peaceful and hopeful about your organized life? My informal surveys say probably not. My informal surveys say there are parts of your life that are absolutely not organized, not peaceful, and appear to be hopeless. You might have piles of laundry heaped in a hamper and overflowing onto the floor. You have a basket of magazines dated two years ago that you have not touched. The kids' toys might be scattered throughout the house, and your children are yelling at one another about changing the channel on the TV. Your mail tray is stacked high, and you cannot pay all the bills on time this month because you over-spent last month. Your car is making funny noises, and you know it is overdue for an oil change. You missed picking up the dry cleaning because you were dealing with an employee problem at work. Your husband is working late *again* and will not be home in time to cut the grass *again*.

None of us ever has the desire to live the *overwhelmed* life. But here you are, and yes, that is you to some degree. Chances are your neighbor, colleague, best friend, sister-in-law, or just about anyone you know is living that same life. It is not just you and yours who are experiencing the clutter and chaos that comes with a disorganized life. As I said in the introduction, our days are filled with the busyness of managing lives. Taking control of the busyness and managing it *well* is the challenge so many, including you, are facing.

You have tried to get things together; I know you have. The prob- lem is in not knowing how to do that in a way that sticks. I call it "the January syndrome." In January, you make plenty of New Year's resolutions. You want to organize your house. You pin those life hacks on Pinterest. You buy beautiful new storage containers. You clean out your clothes closet, your linen closet, and your pantry. Everything is looking *good*. Life goes on. By May everything is looking *bad*. Off you go; buy brand new storage containers. Or maybe "the January syndrome" happens like this for you: the thought of cleaning any closet is simply overwhelming. You say a thankful prayer that *closets have doors*. There—no further action needed.

If either scenario describes you, then I also know that it is not just your closets that need organizing. I am pretty sure your bank account, your relationships, and your family life are filled with clutter and chaos. I also know that when your environment is filled with clutter and chaos, you are not living the life of your dreams. Your heart knows it, too, and it aches. You know there is much more to life than managing clutter and chaos. You were meant for more.

The good news is you have picked up this book. The notebook meeting is the tool you need to organize your life and find your dreams again. It is different than anything you have tried before. It will conquer "the January syndrome." You will organize your life and start living your dreams, no matter what month it is. *Let's get started.*

IN THE BEGINNING

What you are about to read here is just a little peek into how the notebook meetings started years ago. My husband, David, and I had our first official notebook meeting on April 17, 2005. We were not married at the time. This is what we wrote:

> *We commit to meeting with each other and our notebook*
> ***every other*** *Sunday after church. If for some reason we*
> *can't meet at our scheduled time, we commit to meeting*
> *the next Sunday evening. Our purpose is to seek the heart*

*of God about the issues on our list, to grow deeper in love,
to gain a better understanding of each other and ourselves,
and to develop action plans about our lives together.*

Did you see the words **every other** in bold? Read on. Since that initial entry many years ago, David and I have continued to have notebook meetings. When I do the math, it is far from the original "every-other-Sunday" schedule we had so zealously declared. What happened? Life. We busied ourselves not only with the usual tasks—laundry, grocery shopping, yard work—but also with the *extras*—planning a wedding, moving into a new house, starting new jobs, experiencing the death of family members, putting kids through college, building a deck on our house, moving again, and so on. You and I will always have these types of events that will continue to happen.

What else happened? We continued to have our notebook meetings! We managed all the life events I just described to you in ways we could never have done without the notebook meetings. We also began to experience the vision we wrote down in that first meeting. *We continued to seek the heart of God about the issues on our list; we grew deeper in love; we gained a better understanding of each other and ourselves, and we continued to develop action plans about our life together.* We did all of this with our notebook meetings. If you are a family of one or a family of ten, you can do it, too.

YOUR MOUNTAINTOP MOMENTS

Now it is time to focus for a moment on *your dreams and goals.* Yes, even if you have stored those dreams away for a long time, I want you to bring them back to consciousness. What are those flashes of greatness that you hold dearly inside? Perhaps the dreams seem so far away that you have to really reach down deep to touch them again. We all have these dreams. I call them *mountaintop moments.* You and I have visions of *mountaintop living,* even though you may not call it that. We know in our hearts there are goals we want to accomplish and places we want to go with our lives that are *better and higher* than where we are now. Even if you are generally satisfied with your current state of existence, you can always create a vision of going higher. What is in your vision? Take a look at this list:

- A career accomplishment
- More money
- An educational degree
- Better health
- An intimate marriage
- A happy family
- A dream house
- An enlarged circle of friends
- A more active life of serving others
- A published book

Or, perhaps you are far away from even thinking about these grander visions of your dream life. Maybe you are simply seeking a clean house, kids that don't scream at one another, or time to exercise. If that is where you are, then we will set your sights on these visions for now. Keep going; there is great hope ahead.

Starting right now, you and I are heading toward your *mountaintop moments.* These are the ideas you have of living in a higher and better place, of reaching goals that are beyond you right now. As you use the notebook-meeting process, you will reach these mountaintop moments. You absolutely can reach every one of them. *And then there is more...*

If you continue to use the notebook-meeting process, you will discover that whenever you reach one mountaintop, you will find other mountaintops within sight. *You don't have to settle for one mountaintop.* They are all possible. You will reach mountaintop moments you have not even considered yet. Yes, they are waiting for you. But let me be clear about something before your anxiety increases. I am not talking about a state of eternal dissatisfaction with reaching a goal or the unending pursuit of perfection that drives you on a stress-filled endless journey. What I am describing is your desire to grow toward the greater good. As you use the notebook-meeting process and begin reaching your mountaintop moments, you will realize: "If I can do *this*, then I can do *that*, as well. If I can achieve this dream, then I can achieve many other dreams, also."

> *Reaching a mountaintop moment will inspire you*
> *to keep going to your next mountaintop moment.*

Yes, when you reach a mountaintop moment, you will desire other mountaintop moments and realize they are within your reach. What I also know, as one who has lived the notebook-meeting process, the mountaintop moments you will desire will be the *ones that matter for the greater good.* You *will* know this later. Keep reading.

THE PROCESS

As David and I continued to have our notebook meetings over the years, it became clear to me that our process needed to be shared with others. Writing the book you are now holding has been my work in progress for a number of years. It is *one* of my mountaintop moments.

Now it is time for you to have this gift that was given to us. It is time for you to start your own notebook meetings.

In the beginning years of the notebook meetings, David and I did not have the framework that I describe in the following chapters. I had to recreate the process in a workable format with fill-in-the-blank templates so I could successfully share the process with you. Throughout the book I will give you more glimpses and excerpts to reveal how the notebook-meeting process developed for us.

The process I have created, with David's help, can be used by anyone who reads this book and who consistently **chooses** to have the notebook meetings. Please hear me clearly on this next point: I cannot do the work for you. You have to be intentional about bringing change to your life. I know you are ready. I know you can do this. You have already tried other strategies, but they just did not work. The notebook-meeting process works.

I discovered different parts of the process at different times in my life. When I look back at the years before I started the notebook meetings, what strikes me most is that I did not know how to really live with *intention and purpose.*

I just lived, and sometimes, I did not live well.

I finished school, found a job, got married, had a beautiful daughter, cleaned my house every Saturday morning, and bought groceries every Saturday afternoon. That is what I saw others do before me, so I figured that was the way. It was like I was on autopilot with no sense of how I wanted my life to be. I was simply reacting to the needs that came with managing lives. I had no direction, and I did not really know I needed any. I thought I was doing things well.

Life had more in store for me, and it has so much more to offer you as well. During those years that I was just living through the days, I regret that I missed out on opportunities. I missed learning with my then husband how to have an intimate marriage in which two partners help each other grow stronger together. I missed creating great family experiences with my daughter, developing strong friendships, exploring new careers, and learning how to serve others better. It was long after my marriage failed that I kept hearing my heart say I had so much more to learn, more to do, more to experience, and more to offer those who matter to me most. Life started teaching me the lessons *that matter for the greater good.* I had glimpses of living a life that was higher and better than where I currently was. I realized I needed to do the work to find all the good that I had been missing, *the good that really matters.*

I did not learn all of the lessons at once, of course. Neither will you. The lessons came to me like pieces of a puzzle. I am sure life is doing that for you as well. If you take time to look, you will find that your own puzzle pieces are lying all around you. You have missed opportunities just like I had. Your puzzle pieces might be hidden right now, but you are going to find them. The notebook-meeting process will help you pick up the pieces of your puzzle and put them together to create a better life.

THE PUZZLE PIECES

As you read more about the notebook-meeting process, you will learn it involves steps that fit together to help you live a life that is intentional, purposeful, and headed toward the greater good. Let me give you a peek at one of the steps. It involves bringing more organization to your life. You will hear more about this later in the book, too.

For now I want to plant a seed in you that will start growing. I want to give you a vision of the possibilities that lie ahead.

In my early years as an independent adult, I didn't really think about being organized, especially not on paper. I thought everybody lived like I lived. Life just happened, and it kept coming, day after day. I went to work, paid my bills, and managed my life the best I could. I did not save every piece of paper I should have saved, and I did not have my life filed away in a drawer. I did not have an event calendar posted in my kitchen, nor did I keep an ongoing to-do list. So I made plenty of last-minute trips to the grocery store, rarely mailed birthday cards on time, frequently would pay a bill late, and once or twice, I'd been known to lose my keys. OK, so maybe deep down I knew I needed to be more organized. I think secretly I really wanted to be a good list maker. Why secretly? Well, on the surface I certainly would never let anyone *know* I was not organized. I always appeared to be on top of and ahead of all matters. Being organized meant you were a really smart, good person, right? Sometimes I tried. I was a scrap-paper list maker. I made the kind of lists you scribble quickly on the back of something, and then it mysteriously ends up under the front seat of your car.

Well, during one important "season" of my life, it happened. I was about to buy a house on my own, and the responsibilities of completing that process were overwhelming. I remember *in just one day*, near closing day, I participated in thirty phone calls between my realtor, mortgage broker, house inspector, and movers just to coordinate the final steps. I *had* to write everything down. I became a list maker of the highest order. I made lists in categories, *and* I added time schedules to the tasks on my lists. At that time in my life, I had no one else to remember things for me. I had no one else to do things for me. Lists became necessities.

My life changed. I knew I had discovered one of the best things ever. It was a very important puzzle piece that would later become an integral part of my notebook meetings.

And then, I learned about *goals.*

I do not really remember my initial exposure to the earth-shattering concept of having goals. I do remember reading about goal setting in a very unique resource, the *Simple Truths* library. If you have ever been exposed to the *Simple Truths* library, you have probably read Brian Tracy's book, *Eat That Frog.* In it, Brian references a study that focused on goal setting: "Only about 3 percent of adults have clear, written goals." Only 3 percent? Brian goes on to write that "these people accomplish five or ten times more" than those who never take the time *to write out exactly what they want.*

After I read that statement in his book, I was a little exhausted, to tell you the truth. I remember thinking, "I don't really want to do five or ten times more than I'm doing now." Then it sank in: he said they accomplish more. He did not say they were able do more. He meant that if I have ten unwritten things to do on my *unwritten* list, and someone else has a written list of those same ten things to do, you know who would cross off all ten on her list—way before I do my first load of laundry. Did you get that?

Well, that's it, I thought. Just write all my goals down. Bam! Another part of the puzzle.

David and I do that in our notebook meetings. We write it all down. And guess what? We accomplish more than ever before, and we live our lives more intentionally and more purposefully.

We want the same for you.

Making lists and setting goals are just some of the puzzle pieces to the notebook-meeting process. All of our lives are busy enough. I do not want to put more on my list. I do not want you to put more on your list. Instead, finish reading and working through this book, and schedule your first notebook meeting. Follow the process that David and I discovered as we set out to seek the heart of God about the issues on our list: to grow deeper in love, to gain a better understanding of ourselves and each other, and to develop action plans about our lives together. If you are a family of one or a family of ten, keep reading about the process. Learn about my puzzle pieces. They will fit with some of yours, I am sure. It is time for you to have a notebook meeting. Start putting your puzzle pieces together.

Overarching Team Goal of Print Notebook Meeting

CHAPTER TWO

WHY WRITE?

Healing is coming.

Heart to Hand to Pen to Paper

The title of this book is not *The Computer Meeting*. No, it is not *The Tablet Meeting*, either. And no, it is certainly not called *The Smartphone Meeting*. The title of this book is *The Notebook Meeting* for a very important reason. Every time you have a notebook meeting, you will write about it in a notebook. Yes, that is what the name means. I will never direct you to type it on your PC, Mac, laptop, tablet, or make notes on your smartphone. I want you to write everything in a notebook.

I am standing strong on this request. Just go with it.

When you start to have your notebook meetings consistently, you will quickly discover what a precious, precious time it can be. Your notebook meetings will be filled with constructive discussions or thoughts about changing your life for the better. During your meetings you will be talking and writing about doing life differently and in

13

ways you have not yet considered. You will learn more about yourself and your family, you will grow together, you will make plans for your mountaintop moments, and then you will reach those higher places. Recording all of this with your heart and hand using a pen and paper in a notebook will be a highlight of the journey. Your notebook will become a family treasure, a journal of managing life on your terms.

Your notebook will be a celebration in writing
of reaching your mountaintop moments.

Yes, you are right. Your notebook will be a keeper.

FINDING YOUR NOTEBOOK

So, you have some homework. It is time for you to take some action and find a notebook. This is your first big step toward preparing for your notebook meetings. First, though, I need to share a little bit about myself to help you get the right mindset for finding your notebook. This history might reveal a little...well, some may call it "nerdiness," but I consider it "thoughtful intention." Some of you will understand exactly what I mean here; some of you will just have to trust me on this.

When I was in college, one of my greatest delights was visiting the bookstore at the beginning of each quarter to get what I needed to start my new classes. Yes, it's true. It was always exciting to find my textbooks, but that wasn't really the *best* part. The highlight of the day came when I headed to pick up *a brand-new notebook*. I loved searching for just the right one. It was always a substantial, two hundred-page, college-ruled one with that special double-wire spiral binding that I knew would never get wacky or come apart. It had at least five sections with pockets on the dividers. I always chose the color that spoke to me at the moment. I also *always* bought a new pen. My favorite pens are fine-point black ones. They write so crisply. One time I bought a pen that was a white plastic one with coral polka dots and some lime-green accents. It made me happy every time I picked it up. I loved keeping notes during class in my notebook. All my materials and thoughts for every class were just there, contained in my notebook.

Whenever I got home with my new notebook and pen during those college years—and when I do it now—my heart races as I prepare to write on the first page. It is somewhat of a ceremony for me. All of those clean, bright white pages are just waiting for my thoughts. They are waiting for all of my *new* thoughts. New thoughts represent endless possibilities. We all need new thoughts and the hope of endless possibilities.

For your notebook meetings you will need your own brand-new notebook, and don't forget a new pen. Maybe it will have polka dots. Yes, you get to experience the feel of the newness. You get to experience the excitement that comes in knowing that you will be writing *great things*. You will be writing great things with great new pens. Does it sound a little corny to you to get all excited about a new notebook and new pen? Could it be that you just have not thought about it like that before? You will now.

After college, I continued the notebook-buying experience to support my journaling habits. This was way before I ever thought about writing *The Notebook Meeting*. Learning to write in a journal was a powerful process that led to tremendous self-discovery. I have written in journals for years. Journaling helps me find who I am and who I want to be. It helps me to heal from the battles of life. Writing in a journal led me to this book.

WHY WRITE?

Writing in a notebook will lift you to a higher place.

Trust me, and go shopping.

You might ask, "Why, oh why, in this day and age, do I have to write? Why can't I type it onto my device and straight into the cloud?" Well, I have a few thoughts about that. First, let me clarify: I am not antidevice. I love my smartphone. I love my iPad. I love my laptop. I am not on the fence about using these devices. In fact, I want to get rid of the fence. We do not have to be on one side or the other when it comes to using devices. Devices are important parts of our lives for many great reasons. We just do not need them to record our notebook meetings.

"Whaaaaaaaaaaat? I can't use my device?" Well, of course you can, if you want. I am not sitting there with you. I will not be at your notebook meetings. I will not see what you are using. I just *strongly recommend* you not use a device to record your notebook meetings. You can use it as a calendar reference, but that is about it. Read on, my friend. There is wisdom and growth ahead.

Here is the truth of the matter: recording your notebook meetings on paper is part of the healing that comes as you work through the notebook-meeting process. "What? I thought I was just organizing my life. What is it that I need to heal?" you say. When you have your notebook meetings, you will figure it out, and *you will write it down*.

Your day-to-day life contains the symptoms of a life that needs healing. The disorganized life is broken in many ways. You are overwhelmed by the clutter and chaos of your life, have no energy to climb out from under it all, have forgotten who you are, have darkened your greatness and your power, and have stopped having long-term vision. I could go on and on with the list, but I believe you recognize yourself

16

already. All of the *busyness* you find yourself in has distracted you from knowing yourself and from reaching your mountaintop moments. You are not in control anymore. The clutter of your life, physical and emotional, directs how you spend your time every day. Your daily chaos decides your direction and directs your path. You have not touched the heart of who you are for such a long time.

Who are you? Have you looked inside lately? It is time to find out. You will not discover yourself again by picking up a sliver of metal and pecking away on the keyboard. Get a notebook. Get a pen. Let your heart do the work. Let the healing begin.

When you start your notebook meetings and begin to record your life with your hand, you will remind yourself that *you are able.* You will remind yourself that *you are important.* You will remind yourself that *you want to rise to a higher place* and that *you have hope that you will make it.* You will remind yourself that *you have desires for mountaintop moments.*

Then you will discover something even greater. The growing and the healing you experience will also happen to all those around you. Your work with the notebook meetings will lead and inspire others. You will help lead them to their mountaintop moments.

*Writing with your heart and hand
with pen to paper will get you there.*

Trust. Hope. Believe.

CHAPTER THREE

YOUR LIFE ASSESSMENTS

Good things will happen when you do the work.

Looking at the Truth

I am compelled to warn you about this next section. It contains some painful truths that are not being said or thought about *enough*. It is time to call it what it is, and I am armed with evidence that is undeniable. Also, I am not one to speak in gentle, soft terms just so this will be easy for you to hear. I do not want this part to be easy. I want it to be painful for you. I want it to hurt so much that you are eager to make big changes in your life.

Before you start, make sure you are in a quiet place with enough time to contemplate what you are about to read. If you cannot make that happen right now, come back to this later. This is an important life matter. I will start with the simple and concrete. Then I will jump into the messy turmoil that only you can fix.

No, forget that.

I am jumping right into the messy, hard truth. You are the only one who can fix this. Not me, not your best friend, not even your pastor or therapist can fix this. This one is up to you. If you read this section, and say, "Well, that isn't me; my life isn't like *that*," then great. I hope that for you. But if it is you, it is time to acknowledge the truth.

You are living the distracted life.

The distracted life is a very lame excuse
for not doing the hard work
to take your life to a better, higher place.

For whatever reasons—and the reasons are not really important here—you are avoiding being authentic and intentional about living. No, you *are not* intentional about living; you just let life happen to you. The distracted *busyness* of managing day-to-day life—yes, the *busy-ness*—is now the central core of your existence.

This is one of those moments
to think about what you just read.

OK, let me give you another hard way to think about it. You can no longer say that spirituality, love, family, personal growth, health, relationships, or whatever good thing you can think of is at the core of your being. *Distracted busyness* is your core of existence. Distracted busyness is at the center of all you do. Distracted busyness is your sun, and all you do is spin mindlessly around it every day.

It is time to stop. You know that you want more than this. You know that your life's purpose is greater than what you are giving it now. It is time to stop. It is time to lay down the old, messy life and walk forward to better. No need to look back. Just keep moving forward.

THE CLUTTER AND THE CHAOS

I have used this term in paragraphs before, and you will read it again in paragraphs to come. As my husband David would say, this term has a *meta-message*. It has a greater intended meaning than the obvious of the tangible clutter and chaos that you may see in your environment. When I use the term clutter and chaos, I am referring to anything in your life that has negativity, confusion, and discontentment with it, tangible or not.

The clutter could absolutely be those physical things in your environment that make you cringe every time you see them: an overflowing closet, a cabinet of plastic containers that fall out onto the counter, your desk at work, or a refrigerator that needs cleaning. The clutter could also be those intangibles that are taking space and energy that could be used for goodness and creativity: your procrastination in making a much-needed doctor's appointment; 357 e-mails in your inbox at work, involvement in a negative relationship with a friend, coworker, or significant other; or the current balances on your credit cards. In the pages ahead you will focus on the clutter and chaos that is keeping you from reaching your mountaintop moments.

The work ahead will be hard.
All good work is.
It will be worth everything you give it.

REACTIVE LIFE VS. PROACTIVE LIFE

In order to change the way you have been passively living in the chaos and clutter of your distracted busyness, you have to look at it from the practical and concrete viewpoint to understand it. When you recognize your daily cycle of creating more clutter and chaos (this means the emotional as well as the physical), then you will be able to stop it!

You will be able.

One way I think about it is to call it *the reactive life vs. the proactive life*. I love that word *proactive*. It implies so many upbeat, positive qualities. Looking ahead, making plans, and being prepared for future events is being *proactive*. It involves taking the initiative, being preemptive, and having vision. Not looking ahead, not making plans, and not being prepared for anything is *reactive*. The reactive life is passive. I do not even want to write about it. But I will.

The Reactive Life:
- Birthday cards? Usually late. (This one still gets me.)
- Bills? Always paying late fees.
- Groceries? Frequent inconvenient trips to the store.
- Looking for that shirt that completes your outfit? Didn't get washed yet.
- Dinner? Fast food again. No time or food to cook.
- Free time? None available.
- Projects at work? Missed the deadline again.
- Stress level of everyone in the family? Off the charts.
- Guilt level? High.

There is nothing positive, productive, efficient, peaceful, or healthy about living the reactive life. In the reactive life, you are not in control of how your time and days are spent. Instead, you are controlled minute by minute by whatever pops up. You wake up without a plan for the day and start reacting to the distractions around you. You give your time to things that do not move your life forward. The reactive life creates more foothills of clutter and chaos that obscure the paths to your mountaintop moments. You become even more overwhelmed than the day before because the cycle just continues.

Let me give you a small glimpse of how this happens. Read slowly because you are about to get a little queasy as you recognize yourself. Imagine it is Saturday morning. Or it could be Tuesday night. Hmmm, definitely Thursday during lunch. Instead of paying your bills online, checking next month's calendar for upcoming events, or calling your mom because it is her birthday, you hop on Facebook. Bam, there goes a good hour or more because you also answered or sent twenty-three text messages while you were checking all the new posts. Then, of course, you have to check your e-mail. Bam, there goes another forty-five minutes. We have become a society that promotes attention-deficit disorder by allowing the activity on our devices to control our lives. You jump from one topic to the next in seconds without giving it any focus. And I just got started describing only part of your day. I have not yet mentioned watching reality TV.

What are you doing?
Quit being mindless about your life.

Like I said before, I do not even want to keep writing about it. It is an awful existence that many do not want to acknowledge. It involves those awful terms like self-gratification, narcissism, self-indulgence, laziness, etc. Ooooh, yuck. Let's change the topic.

The Proactive Life:
- Your day? You have a plan.
- Your kids? They feel secure because mom's got this life thing down.
- Your job? You're headed for a promotion!
- Your heart? Alive and thriving.
- Your creativity? Overflowing.
- Smile? Look at your face.
- The details? Hey, the proactive life is what the notebook meetings are all about. I have more than just a paragraph about the proactive life. I can hardly wait for you to get there!

THE GOOD STUFF

It's time to learn how to make events in life work for you, not against you. You can learn how to be the manager *of your life* instead of being managed *by your life*. The notebook-meeting process will lead you to a lifestyle of being *proactive* instead of *reactive* for all daily life matters that come to you. When you are *proactive*, you are prepared to manage both the expected events and the unexpected ones. You are not there—*yet*.

As you work through the notebook-meeting process, start looking for those moments when you realize "OK, I've got this! I know how to handle this crisis, change, or minor event because I've learned how to have a plan. I know where I want to go and what I want to do." It will be a new way of living that will empower you. You will have the emotional strength and creativity to take on whatever comes your way.

You will direct your own steps from a place of confidence, clarity, and vision.

Trust that you will get there.
The day will come. Just keep doing the work.

Before you can get to that clear, confident place, though, you have to relinquish the *reactive* lifestyle that helped you accumulate the clutter and create the chaos around you. Remember, when I talk about clutter and chaos, it means the emotional and relational clutter and chaos as well as the physical stuff around you. Relinquishing that lifestyle means you are ready to change your current situation.

You are ready to move the foothills that are in your way as you journey toward your mountaintops. Removing the clutter and taming the chaos will open the floodgates of your creativity, energy, and forward vision. You will have physical and mental room to get busy with the life of your dreams! You will make clear the paths to your higher self. You will reach your mountaintop moments. Right now the clutter and chaos, in whatever forms they may be, are blocking your paths.

THE AGENDA

To be successful with the notebook-meeting process, you must always have an agenda for your meetings. This is a list of discussion items that you will prepare *before* each meeting. (You will find a template for this in a later chapter.) This simple step of creating an agenda *before* you meet will soon be a habit that will become a natural part of your lifestyle as you have more notebook meetings. The agenda is the working point for each meeting. During your actual notebook meeting, you will use the agenda to create action plans for improving your current situation. You and your family will brainstorm steps and devise plans for tackling whatever is blocking your paths to living the life you desire. No need to worry; these steps will become clear as you work through the process.

Before I go on, let me remind you that if you are single and wanting to follow the notebook-meeting process, everything I write is for you, also. The notebook-meeting process is for any*one*, not just families. You will create your own agenda. You will have your own notebook meetings. You will develop your own action plans. Please do not stop reading just because I use the word family or partner. This process is about helping any*one* find and live the life of your dreams. Remember, whether you are a family of one or a family of ten, a small-business owner or a student, a rising professional or a grandmother, the note-book-meeting process is for *you*.

NOTEBOOK-MEETING PREPARATION PART ONE

How to Create the Agenda: Life Assessments

The following assessments are the work you need to do to be ready for your first notebook meeting. I made a list below so you will know what is ahead. Check them off here when complete. The work you are about to complete on the following assessments is what you will use to create the agenda for your notebook meeting. You will read more about the agenda in chapter six. Do the following assessments first! For every assessment I list here, I am including a blank template in the pages ahead for you to use.

_____ Assessment #1: My List of the Obvious
_____ Assessment #2: Digging Deeper
_____ Assessment #3: Rising Higher
_____ Assessment #4: Grab the Future

To create a meaningful agenda, you must first have a clear vision of what is truly going on in your life. Here is where you take a long, hard look at the obstacles that are keeping you (and your family) from reaching your mountaintop moments. You must make an honest assessment of where and who you are. A thorough self-assessment is crucial to creating an agenda that will matter.

This self-assessment is a continual part of the process, and it has to happen before each notebook meeting. Once you develop this skill of looking at your life in order to create your agenda, it will become automatic, something you will do later without effort. It will become part of your nature to always know the "big-picture view" of your life.

With **Assessment #1: My List of the Obvious**, the items you write about will be the things that are front and center in your house or any part of your life that are draining you of your physical and mental energy right now. These things are the foothills of clutter and chaos that you have to conquer. For some of us, as I described before, there are actual foothills of laundry, junk mail, or toys that are out of control. So, take a good look at your physical environment: yard work not done, a basement that needs cleaning, or piles of magazines sitting in the corner. Or perhaps your clutter and chaos is financial: unpaid bills, no funds for the future, or unexpected car repairs. It might also be social, emotional, or vocational: negative relationships, depression, anger, an uninspiring job, no job, or too many obligations at church.

Whatever the sources of your clutter and chaos, know that they are obstacles in your path. They are foothills that you must first overcome before you reach your mountaintop moments. The clutter and chaos of daily life will overwhelm you quickly if you do not give it your attention and create a plan for managing it well. The notebook-meeting process will lead you to create such a plan. I promise.

So, it is time to do the preliminary work that will lead to creating the agenda for your first notebook meeting. On the following pages, I am including two work sheets for you to complete, or you can recreate these in your own notebook. Remember, there is power in writing it all down. Start first with **Assessment #1: My List of the Obvious**, of course.

ASSESSMENT #1: MY LIST OF THE OBVIOUS

This assessment will help you identify what is taking your energy the most right now. Look around. I know you have already thought about this as you were reading this chapter. Is your pantry out of control? Is your clothes closet overflowing into the bedroom? How tall are your stacks of mail? Has your lawn grown into a field of weeds? Does your basement need cleaning? Whenever you get to the work sheet, please write down whatever physical chaos is overwhelming you right now.

This is where you start. These are the smaller foothills that are blocking your path. These foothills of chaos, minor or major, can take an inordinate amount of energy. How many days have you walked through your garage and muttered the same negative self-talk you muttered yesterday? You are losing energy by not taking action, energy you would rather have for the greater matters in life. These foothills of clutter also block *your vision*. You cannot even see the possibility of reaching your mountaintop moments.

Let me stop you here for a moment and remind you of some truths you already know. *We all have things we can improve.* If you do not honestly look at your life and tackle the clutter and chaos, *whatever it may be*, you will not get to your mountaintop moments. When you get to the assessments, please keep digging. Are your finances in order? Do you really know? How is your extended family? Do you have to check a device before you can answer that? I am sure by now your mind is racing, and you are ready to complete **Assessment #1: My List of the Obvious.**

Before you go, I have another truth to share with you. This one comes from David. *You cannot unpack it all at once.* What he means is that this beginning work you are doing does not have to tackle *everything*. It is too hard to make the perfect list that touches every area of your life. You get to decide what you want to give your attention to first. Choose *some*. My encouragement to you is to start just with the obvious energy zappers. Tackle the things you have been procrastinating the most.

Need some more encouragement and clarity? Let me show you what David and I wrote in the early days. As you read, please know that we did not have the framework I write about here. To write this book, I had to look back through our process and recreate our method so that I could deliver it to you. Do I wish I had the templates earlier? No, not really. As I described in an earlier chapter, I believe the process was revealed to me like pieces of a puzzle. I had to learn how to put the notebook-meeting puzzle together so I could write this book for you. I had to live through the process to understand how important and life changing the notebook meeting is. I want you to have the best of the process now.

Excerpt from David and Stuart's Notebook Meeting
May 15, 2005

Note: This was five months before we got married. We had separate
houses! I wrote as we talked. David and I always used one notebook
together. We never completed any of this process separately.

If we had had this **Assessment #1: My List of the Obvious** template, this is what we would have completed.

Assessment #1: My List of the Obvious

MY CLUTTER AND CHAOS CATEGORIES:	THE SPECIFICS:
Home	David does not have enough food in his house when his boys come over.
Family	Communication problems—we're not available to each other; we're not talking about difficult, important topics. We'd like to have our kids at David's house together.
Health	We're not dedicating enough time to working out.
Work	We need to coordinate our schedules. We don't want to live our lives separately.
Social Life	We're scheduling things without checking with each other.
Emotional Life	We're not focused on our relationship.

Now it's your turn. I'm giving you another sample on the following page just to help bring more clarity. Following the sample is a blank one for you to complete. Don't stop now! Just write it all down.

Assessment #1: My List of the Obvious: (sample)

MY CLUTTER AND CHAOS CATEGORIES:	THE SPECIFICS:
Family	It's hard to manage kids' schedules and cook dinner. Kids are disrespectful. My husband and I aren't communicating well.
Home	Garage needs cleaning. We need a new refrigerator. Deck needs staining. Kids' bedrooms are a mess. My scrapbooking projects are not finished.
Health	Health is not where I want to be. I'm always tired.
Work	I want a career change. I want to go back to school.
Social Life	I don't spend enough time with friends.
Emotional Life	Stressful—my parents are struggling with their health

The next one is yours! You can add whatever categories come to mind.

Assessment #1: My List of the Obvious:

MY CLUTTER AND CHAOS CATEGORIES:	THE SPECIFICS:
Home	
Family	
Health	
Work	
Social Life	
Emotional Life	

What you just created is so important! You did it! You took a look at your life, and it did not scare you away. Please keep going! You must dig a little deeper. Digging deeper and completing these work sheets will bring clarity. You cannot know it now, but it will happen. I promise.

ASSESSMENT #2: DIGGING DEEPER

Digging deeper means you will now create a list of the sources of your clutter and chaos that *are not so obvious*. You can do it. *Keep reading, and keep writing it down.* Like before with **Assessment #1: My List of the Obvious,** you will find a sample from me of the **Assessment #2: Digging Deeper** work sheet. Then you will find a blank one for yourself. Before you jump to the next work sheet, let's get your mind focused. Give me the quick, off-the-top-of-your-head, first-word-you-think-of answer to this question:

How would you describe your life right now? _____

Busy? Full of conflict? Broken? Successful? Scattered? Whatever the answer, wherever you are, it is time to take a look at what your answer truly means.

Where are you?

Look at the sample **Assessment #2: Digging Deeper** work sheet on the next page. I have filled it with notes to give you an idea of how you may want to complete it. Write down whatever comes to your mind. Yes, you may be repeating things you just wrote. There is no one right way. This is a *work sheet.* It is one step in this process of getting you to your mountaintop moments. Every step of the notebook-meeting process has great meaning. Take the time to write very thoughtful, purposeful notes. This is your life. You have to do the work to answer your own questions.

of the **Assessment #2: Digging Deeper** work

he blank one on page 36, or record this in your

Assessment #2: Digging Deeper: (sample)

1. How do you describe your life?	2. What makes it so?	3. Prioritize your answers for the previous column. Where do you want to direct your attention first? Choose as many as you like.	4. Looking at what you wrote for column 3, write why you chose these as priorities.
Busy	Work overload, chores at home, too many commitments at church, kids' activities, caring for parents	Kids' activities Chores at home	Driving time takes away from other things We scramble for clean clothes House is too dirty for guests
Full of conflict	Relationship with spouse, kids, extended family, boss	Relationship with spouse Relationships with kids	We argue a lot Kids and I yell at each other I don't want to live like that
Broken	Depressed, divorced, addicted, abused, unemployed,	Depression Unemployment	All I think about (Please see special note at the end of this chapter.)
Successful, looking for what's next	Happy family, great career, good health, growing spiritually	Spiritual growth Happy family	Want to give & serve more Want to enlarge family's dreams

Scattered	Disorganized at home, making mistakes at work, had a crisis	Organizing my house Getting past the crisis (car wreck, need $ for repairs)	This is where all of my energy is being spent right now

Looking at your life like that can be exhausting. Or perhaps it is energizing! My guess is that it is a little of both. Getting to a mountaintop moment is hard work. *It is worth everything you give it.* Now it is your turn.

Assessment #2: Digging Deeper:

1. How do you describe your life?	2. What makes it so?	3. Prioritize your answers for the previous column. Where do you want to direct your attention first? Choose as many as you like.	4. Looking at what you wrote for column 3, write why you chose these as priorities.

Celebrate for a moment the work you just did.

It probably took a lot of time and energy to complete the work sheet. Whenever you dig deeper, you have to look at some difficult areas of your life. I am sure you had to have some honest moments that hurt. You had to feel some heartache.

That is why you are here. That is why you have this book in your hand. *You are ready to look at the hard things and do the hard work.* If you keep going with the notebook-meeting process, you will overcome the foothills that are in your way, and *you will reach your mountaintop moments.*

> *Special Note: If you are someone who describes your life as broken, it may be time to acknowledge that you need help beyond the scope of this book. If you are depressed, addicted, suffering from abuse, or experiencing any such challenge, I encourage you to continue the notebook-meeting process and to please reach out to a professional or an organization that can help you with your specific challenge. Health and growth come to us in many different forms. The notebook-meeting process is a great tool for moving forward, but you may need additional support on your journey.*

NOTEBOOK-MEETING PREPARATION, PART TWO

The following steps are optional for right now, but you must come back to them later. Read this page right now for instructions. Then decide if you are ready for part two or not.

If the work you just completed on **Assessments #1 and #2** is beginning to overwhelm you, it's OK to decide to not do this next phase right now. Truthfully, you might already have the makings of a pretty full agenda for your first actual notebook meeting from the work you just did with **Assessments #1 and #2.** You can note the date below and jump ahead to the next chapter, *knowing you will come back to this.* Sometimes, you have to focus your best efforts on clearing the clutter and chaos that are currently in your life before you can look to making plans about your future. Doing the work now to clear the messy stuff out will give you more clarity, energy, and vision to devote to reaching your mountaintop moments later.

You can choose right here to not do the next assessments and instead jump ahead to the next chapter. No worries. What you will continue to learn about the notebook-meeting process will help you direct your current energy to clearing the obvious foothills that are blocking your path to a better life. When you have had a few meetings and started some action plans, then you will be ready to come back to **Assessments #3: Rising Higher** and **Assessment #4: Grab the Future.**

Write down today's date:

Write the date four months from now:

Go to this date on your calendar and put a reminder to "Read and do **Assessments #3 and #4** in chapter three of *The Notebook Meeting*." Good. All done for now. Jump ahead to the next chapter! Yes, really! Or, if you want to continue at full speed with the notebook-meeting process, read on, my friend!

———— **Assessment #3: Rising Higher**
———— **Assessment #4: Grab the Future**

Continuing with this part of completing the preliminary work for your first notebook-meeting agenda requires two important actions. First, you will look to the future and record which upcoming events will need your attention. Secondly, you get to start dreaming a little. Remember the mountaintop moments I talked about in chapter one? Those dreams you have not touched in a while? Well, they are about to become a little more solid. You are about to work them into real life. Here is how the dreaming works: stand on your tippy toes and look over the foothills (like the laundry, debt, or negative relationships) in your way. Set your eyes on the other side of the foothills, and look to the mountaintops beyond. Gaze at the future, and imagine yourself there. When your foothills of clutter and chaos are gone, where do you want to direct your energy?

What are your mountaintop moments?
What are your dreams?

Have you always wanted to go back to school? Are you interested in a different career? Do you want to start your own business? Do you want to publish a book? What home improvement projects are on your wish list? When your vision includes your family, what are those mountaintop moments? Do you see a family that no longer yells at one another? Do you see the family that works together to complete the household chores? Or maybe your vision hits a little closer to your heart: Are you seeing a family that *wants* to spend time with one another? Is there a dream vacation you really want to make happen? The dreams and the possibilities are endless. There are many mountaintop moments waiting for you.

Sometimes it's best to choose only a few dreams to come into focus before you get overwhelmed. Later, after working through some notebook meetings and reaching a few mountaintop moments, *you can choose more.* It will always be up to you. Yes, it's time for another work sheet. On the **Assessment #3: Rising Higher** and **Assessment #4: Grab the Future** work sheets, you will list your mountaintop moments, and you will list events in the immediate future that need your attention. Looking ahead and making plans for future events is being *proactive.* This is where you start directing your life instead of letting life direct you. It is time to give it a try.

Here is more good news: just as I told you when you started the other assessments, these, too, will become second nature to you after you start the notebook meetings. You will not have to come back to these work sheets every time you have a meeting unless you want. The work sheets are designed to help you learn the notebook-meeting process. These are your starting points. We are using them for practice.

On the next page you will find the sample **Assessment #3: Rising Higher** and **Assessment #4: Grab the Future** work sheets. On the pages that follow these, you will find blank ones for you to use.

Assessment #3: Rising Higher: (Sample)

1. What are my mountaintop moments?	2. What do I need to get there?
Home Having a craft room	Redo the guest bedroom.
Family Having Sunday dinners with all of my family	Talk to my sister-in-law; plan it!
Health Change my lifestyle to consistently get more sleep.	I don't know yet.
Work Submit my project proposal.	Make an appointment with my boss.
Social Life Join a hiking group.	Call the park to get info, or search online.
Spiritual Life Join a bible study group.	Ask at church.

Assessment #4: Grab the Future: (Sample)

1. List upcoming events:	2. What do you need to handle it?
Birthdays Husband's	Arrange family celebration, and purchase gift.
Family Dentist appts for children Plan vacation.	Let everyone know; check calendar. Save $; decide on trip specifics.
Home/Car Need oil change	Schedule this.
Social Tailgating party	Decide menu; make list of supplies.

Now it's your turn! Use the following blank one, or recreate your own in your notebook.

Assessment #3: Rising Higher

1. What are my mountaintop moments?	2. What do I need to get there?
Home	
Family	
Health	
Work	
Social Life	
Spiritual Life	

Assessment #4: Grab the Future

1. List upcoming events:	2. What do you need to handle it?

Once again, *take a moment to celebrate the work you just did!*

Are you feeling energized? You're getting closer to *proactively* managing your life instead of allowing life to manage you. *Congratulations!* You're almost ready to schedule your first notebook meeting!

CHAPTER FOUR

ALMOST THERE

Your life is about to change.

The Big Picture

Congratulations, again! You have completed the hardest part, the life assessments. The good news is that you do not have to be overwhelmed with whatever you wrote. Taking inventory of your clutter and chaos is the first step in controlling it. You are on the right path. Remember, you are taking steps toward a life of being *proactive*, not *reactive*. You will continue to make choices that will lead you to the other side of the clutter. Now, it is time to start moving those foothills of clutter out of the way.

The more you read this book, you are probably recognizing that the steps of the notebook meeting are very methodical. You will soon discover, if you have not already, that I have incorporated some very important business principles for conducting your notebook meetings. In addition to the effective practices of *making lists* and *agendas*, you will be writing *action plans* with *methods for accountability* and *dates for completion*. You will also end each meeting by *scheduling* the subsequent meeting at a date and time that works for everyone in attendance. Oh yes, I just heard the click, click, clicks of all the switches. The lightbulbs are popping. You are getting the picture, aren't you?

Let me put that into list form, just to be clear. The components of a notebook meeting are:

_____ A notebook for recording everything
_____ The agenda (explained in chapter six)
_____ Action plans
_____ Dates for accountability/completion of plans
_____ Scheduled date/time of next notebook meeting

If you did indeed just experience a lightbulb moment and are feeling oh so confident and energized about getting started with your meetings, I want to encourage you to *not start just yet.* Keep reading! Even if you quickly grasp the big-picture view of the notebook meetings, I want you to keep doing the work here, and finish this book. There are *subtle, yet very powerful* moments I do not want you to miss.

I am excited for you as I think of what lies ahead in your journey. If you simply start having meetings without understanding the rest of the process, you may find yourself...well, stuck. Once you start the notebook meetings, it is all about *moving* forward. I want you to know the entire process, so you will keep *moving forward for the greater good.*

THE BIG PICTURE

Whenever someone asks me to explain the notebook meeting, I admit that I struggle to answer the question. I always want to say, "You have to read the book." There is no short-answer way of explaining the entire process. We are in chapter four, and only now am I willing to give you this big-picture overview. The notebook meeting is a process of meetings that can change your life if you are *true to the process*. I hope no one skims this book and thinks he or she can proceed successfully just by having a family meeting. *It is so much more than that.*

So, if you have read everything up to this point, you have an overview of the notebook-meeting process, but you have not started the meetings *yet*. You're almost there. Let me give you a glimpse into the future. You will not believe what lies ahead. Really, it will be hard for you to believe all the goodness that is coming because you have lived in the other stuff so long!

After you have had a few meetings and experience the success of your action plans, your life will take a shift, a jump, or a leap into a new existence. At some point you will have cleared or learned to better manage most of your current clutter and chaos. You then start to make plans to proactively manage the new clutter and chaos, which means you can no longer call it clutter and chaos. Think about it. You will become quite skilled at managing the day-to-day tasks and events because you will have energy, time, and room in your life to do so. Those foothills that are blocking your paths will be gone.

Then the days will be brighter, your heart will be lighter, and you will begin to go after the good stuff. You will go after the dreams that have been on the shelf because all the other stuff was in the way. You will create plans to accomplish those dreams. Then you will reach the point that you can no longer call them dreams because they will be your reality.

When you are living in your new reality (achieved with your magnificent, hard work), then you will realize you are on a higher path. You will be living a life for the greater good. Take a moment to imagine yourself reaching this point. Can you guess what comes next?

47

Think about it! Here it comes: rinse and repeat. Just kidding about the rinse part, but the repeat part will always be part of the process. Every time you go forward with the process, you will be directing your steps toward a higher path that will lead to another dream, another goal, and another mountaintop moment. When you reach one mountaintop moment, you will be ready for the next one.

The notebook-meeting process is without end.

It is a complex, fully active process that can be a challenge to comprehend *until you live it.* You and I were not generally raised to believe we have endless mountaintop moments that are reachable. Our limited view is that we have one distant dream of greatness (winning the lottery?) and that only the really lucky ones get to live a dream life. Well, I have much good news to share with you. The notebook-meeting process is very inclusive.

Everyone can be successful.

THE GREATER GOOD

What exactly is the greater good? How do your success and my success with the notebook-meeting process affect the greater good?

I love the term "the greater good." Who wouldn't? What you do with the notebook-meeting process will change your life for the better. Your goodness will overflow. Your positive energy, creativity, and excitement for life will be part of who you are wherever you go and whatever you do. Others will witness it and be energized as well. You will share the great things that are happening in your life, and you will keep doing great things.

Others will want to do what you are doing. You will lead the way. As a family or a single person, the actions you take in this world affect others, whether you want them to or not. It cannot be avoided. As you begin to have your meetings, you will directly and indirectly help those around you to live the life of their dreams on a higher path. When that happens, it will affect your neighborhood, your community, and your world. When you make your world better, you make my world better.

That is for the greater good.

CHAPTER FIVE

BRING EVERYONE WITH YOU

You CAN bring everyone with you.
You will be a team.

Who Is "Everyone"?

By now you have a "big-picture" idea of some of the most important components of your notebook meetings. Keep that vision in mind. You are about to enlarge it. You are going to learn how to *bring everyone with you*. Who is everyone? Well, the answer to that varies of course. If you are single, you may not want to bring anyone else into the process right now, but keep reading this chapter anyway. You will see the importance of considering others in your life to join you in your notebook meetings. Also, there is a discussion toward the end of this chapter about a surprise component of the notebook meetings. Do not miss this! If you are not single and live with others as a family, they are the ones you will bring with you on this journey. They need it. You all need it as a family.

As I write this, David and I have been married for eleven years, and the notebook meetings are part of who we are. If our children

51

were still living in our house, they would also participate in each of our meetings. Let me repeat what I wrote in the introduction to this book:

For all of us, whether we are a family of one or a family of ten, the day-to-day life events we face are the greatest threats to our happiness, success, and, most importantly, our ability to love one another, especially those we call our own. Our days are filled with the busyness of managing lives. Too often we lay our heads on our pillows at night wondering where the time went, another day spent on activities that do not match the desires of our hearts. If you desire to become more intentional and purposeful about really living your life, it is time to schedule your first notebook meeting.

That is why you need to bring others along. Too many of us have lost our way. It is time to get back on the path of living intentionally *for the greater good.*

TALKING TO OTHERS

Before you can bring others along with you, you must tell them about the process. Like everything else with the notebook meeting, you *need a plan* for approaching others with the notebook-meeting idea. Start by making arrangements to have a meaningful conversation with each person in the house. You can do this one at a time, or you can talk with everyone together. Yes, everyone is included. Everyone can take part in the notebook meetings, and your introduction needs a meaningful conversation held at the right time with the right tone of voice, filled with excitement for the future.

> *Special Note: I know right now there are many families living together in a state of crisis: broken, fighting, hurting, and hopeless. If you are part of one of these families, I am so glad you are reading this book. As I stated in chapter three, I encourage you to reach out to a professional or an organization that can help, and use this book as a resource to help with your healing. I know you want better. You and your family deserve better. If you determine that no one can join you in the notebook meetings right now, then so be it. If the breakdown is between you and your children, then maybe just you and your spouse can work together on the notebook meetings for now. If you are a single mom living in such crisis, you must do the work to heal. This is your journey. Keep moving.*

Right now I am guessing that you are the only one in your family reading this book. You are the one who purchased the notebook and the pen. You are the one who completed the life-assessment work sheets in chapter three. You have all the insights into the process. Congratulations, this makes you the "notebook-meeting manager."

Oh, what an important position you have! You are the one who will gather the troops and enlist their help in changing how your family lives now. You are the one who gets to share the vision with others. You are the one who gets to lead everyone else toward his or her mountaintop moments.

You are also the one who will make sure the notebook meetings happen—in the beginning, that is. Later, others will come to you wanting a meeting. The process is that powerful. *Your family will change for the better.* Everyone will be attracted to the process when they see good happening. In the beginning, you will manage the "team" as you all work toward reaching your mountaintop moments. Later, when the process is solid for all of you, you will not have to convince anyone to join you on the notebook-meeting journey. The process will take care of that.

Everyone wants good, and good will happen.

So how does that work, getting everyone on board? How do you convince them to join in?

You tell the truth.

Maybe your truth sounds like this:

> "Hey honey, I know lately we've been super busy, and things seem to be spiraling out of control. Our lives are very stressful, and we have been arguing more than usual. I don't want us to keep living like this, and I know you don't want it this way either. I have a solution that will help us. When is a good time to talk about an idea I have?"

> "Hey, kids, I know that you don't think you have much say in what happens in our family. I remember last week when you guys said dad and I don't understand you or trust you to do anything. I have a solution that will help us

talk about this and manage everything better. How about we choose a time we can sit down together to talk about some ideas?"

"Hey, sweetie, I know that for years we have dreamed of opening our own shop. I discovered something that will help us make that happen. When can we sit down to talk about it?"

Start thinking about having these conversations with others in your family. Practice in your head using your own words. Think about the ideal time and location to present your ideas. If tension and conflict are always existent in your household, really think hard about what you will say to people who may reject your initial idea. Also know that as the parent, you are the one directing the healing and the change that you want to have in your family. It is time for you to take charge of getting your family on a higher path.

You will notice in the examples above that my language did not give anyone a choice in whether or not to join you. If you use the examples above, you will simply be asking for them to help choose a time to talk. This is *subtle yet powerful.* Think about how you can make it happen. Practice the conversation before you have it with each member of your family. Commit to using a sincere, hope-filled tone of voice. Commit to trying again if someone rejects your initial requests.

SURPRISE COMPONENT OF
THE NOTEBOOK MEETINGS

Are you feeling anxious about the challenge of getting others to join you? Well, I have another component of the notebook meetings that takes the entire process to another level. This surprise component is equally important for single individuals and for families.

The notebook meetings are *not just meetings.*

No, never, never, never have *just a meeting.* Instead, have a notebook-meeting event! Plan a special Saturday morning breakfast or a Sunday afternoon picnic! Have a date with yourself and your notebook at your favorite coffee shop. Combine your meetings with pizza night! Take your notebook and camping chairs to a state park, and circle around! Put your notebook in your backpack, and go on a hike! Sit on the rocks near the river, and let the creativity flow!

I am having flashbacks as I write this because David and I did almost all of the above. *Our meetings are special.* We love this time together. When we meet, we are celebrating the joys of managing our lives and making plans for our futures. We want to make it a special event every time we meet! Planning an event such as those listed above establishes a very positive "anchor" to our notebook meetings. You can do this, too!

Take a moment to think of how you can do that for yourself or your family. Where do your special moments happen? If nothing comes to you right away, then maybe you will be creating these moments now. Choose a spot: a blanket on the living-room floor, a picnic table in the back yard or at the local park, or perhaps you have a favorite family restaurant that will be quiet enough for everyone to hear and talk. You decide!

Then you will add this to your initial invitation:

"I want to schedule a meeting with you. Can we meet this Saturday morning? I'll make a pancake breakfast for us! How does 9:00 sound?"

Then make a sign with all the details, and hang it in the kitchen. Keep talking it up. Get the curiosity and excitement started early!

Well, Notebook-Meeting Manager, are you getting the idea? Yes, you can do this. You can get this started. Remind everyone about the meeting as it draws near. If someone has to reschedule, then everyone reschedules. In the beginning, others may not have the same level of enthusiasm that you do. That will change. When everyone sees the power of the process, they will work hard with you to protect the notebook-meeting schedule. Your passion and your desire for your family to *be better, live better, and do better* will be evident. Others will see that in you. They will want it, too.

Now is the time to look at a calendar and schedule your first notebook meeting. If you all use a calendar app on your devices, then create the first notebook-meeting event (after you get everyone on board), and send the event info to all involved. If you are single, choose a date for your notebook meeting, and enter that on your calendar. I suggest you also print a paper calendar to go with that sign posted in the kitchen! Keep talking about the meeting. Keep talking about those pancakes, and take special orders. Blueberries? Bananas and walnuts? Chocolate chips? If you make it special, they will feel special.

OK, here we go. As soon as you talk with everyone, write the date and time of your first notebook meeting here:

....

Congratulations. You did it!

Now, it is your job to make sure it happens.
How?
Be proactive; start now. Make a list!

MATERIALS/ACTIONS NEEDED
FOR YOUR FIRST NOTEBOOK MEETING:

_____ A notebook and a pen; date for purchasing by (stick to this!)

_____ **Assessment #1: My List of the Obvious**

_____ **Assessment #2: Digging Deeper**

_____ Pancake ingredients (insert your favorite here!)

_____ Reminders for meetings

Please write all of this in your notebook! Take action now!

CHAPTER SIX

THE FIRST NOTEBOOK MEETING

You have done the hard work.
Good is coming.

You Are Ready

Please read this chapter *before* the day of your first notebook meeting. The steps I describe in this chapter are very important for you to read so that the process works powerfully, whether you are single or whether you are a family of more than one. If you are a family of more than one, and you are preparing for others to join you, remember that you have to create the vision for everyone else, unless they have read this book. This chapter will help you see the vision.

If you are single and journeying through the notebook-meeting process by yourself, it might seem that much of this chapter does not address your present situation, but I believe it does. The conversation ahead about communication strategies applies to all life situations, not just notebook meetings. Also, you will read about how to invite others into the notebook-meeting process, which will prepare you for that possibility in the future.

My hope is that you will honor your journey by making each note-book meeting a memorable event, as I describe in chapter five. Resist the temptation to just plow ahead with the paperwork. The notebook-meeting process is not just about completing work sheets. Honor this time in which you are choosing to improve your life. Play some special background music, light your favorite candles, cuddle in your softest blanket, and brew your most calming tea. Commit to always making your notebook-meeting time special. Choose to do that *for yourself.* Follow the steps ahead to make sure you experience the fullness of the process.

START WITH THE END IN MIND

One very important principle of planning anything is to *start with the end in mind.* To have a successful meeting, you must always know where you are going. Here is a quick overview of the components of your first notebook meeting that must be in place before you start. (Yes, a list!)

Components of the First Notebook Meeting:

_____ You have decided on the date and the specifics of the event. If you are inviting others, you have agreed with all involved on a date, time, menu, and location.

_____ If you are preparing food or a meal, have it ready before the meeting begins.

_____ You have a notebook and a pen.

_____ A printed calendar is helpful for planning. If it is printed, everyone can see it.

_____ You completed these assessments from chapter three and have them available:

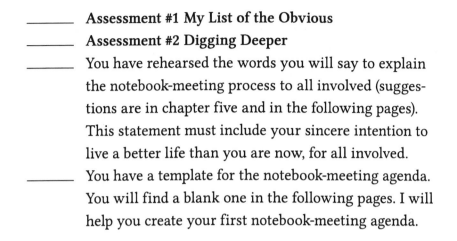

In chapter three, you worked on **Assessment #1: My List of the Obvious** and **Assessment #2: Digging Deeper** *by yourself.* Completing these life assessments by yourself is a necessary step because you are the one who will be leading this process for now. For this first meeting, the first two assessments from chapter three that you completed will provide the road map for the changes you want to happen in your life. *Those assessments contain the foothills of clutter and chaos that are keeping you from reaching your mountaintop moments.*

However, during this first notebook meeting, you will *not* be the only one talking and making decisions. Others will have thoughts and reactions to what you have written. Developing plans to take care of this current clutter and chaos will be a group effort. You will invite others to the conversation, which will promote engagement. Your goal is to allow others to help solve problems and make suggestions. After this first notebook meeting, the others you invite will help you create the new agendas for subsequent notebook meetings. You will read about that later. For now, your job is to make sure you are prepared for your first notebook meeting.

Besides putting the event on the calendar, there are other actions you can take to prepare for a successful notebook meeting. You have already purchased a notebook and pen and completed **Assessment #1** and **Assessment #2** from chapter three. It is time to actually write the agenda. The agenda will help you walk through the meeting every time. The very first notebook-meeting agenda will be different from the agenda for every other notebook meeting to come. The template for your first notebook-meeting agenda is in the following pages. (Keep reading to get to it. I am so excited for you!)

GATHERED TOGETHER

Imagine for a moment that you all have finished the pancakes or the pizza, and everyone is waiting with anticipation to hear your ideas. During the meal, you talked with great excitement about your family's first notebook meeting. Your voice relayed the hope you have that *better days are coming*. As you begin to explain what happens in the notebook meeting to others, I want to encourage you to be very intentional with everything you say. As my husband David explains: "There is great power in words."

GUIDELINES FOR COMMUNICATING WELL

Productive communication will be so important during your entire notebook meeting. Stating some guidelines for talking during your notebook meeting will be crucial. Here are the guidelines I suggest you use.

1. Everyone gets a chance to discuss ideas, but only one person at a time talks without others interrupting.

2. We paraphrase what is said to check for understanding and clarity.
3. We talk with a respectful tone and respectful words.

PARAPHRASING

It will take some practice to fully implement the strategy of paraphrasing as you record your notebook meeting, but it can be such a positive thing to do. When someone makes a contribution, paraphrase what the person said before you write it down. This allows you to check for understanding, and it communicates the message that you are truly listening. This simple act of paraphrasing can change a reluctant participant's level of engagement immediately! Paraphrasing is one of the most important guidelines that you can all agree on for every meeting. Allow everyone to help with the paraphrasing. No matter who is recording the meeting, everyone participates in restating what ever is said.

David conducts parenting seminars, and he uses a powerful example of paraphrasing that shows parents the importance of using this strategy when communicating with children. If you are not a parent and are conducting a notebook meeting with your spouse or partner, I know this example will speak to you as you consider how to successfully implement paraphrasing.

David uses the example of a child's bedtime as a point of contention during a family argument. Your ten-year-old son may complain that his current bedtime of 8:00 p.m. is too early, and he wants to change it to 11:00 p.m. In a heated family argument, a parent's response may be, "Absolutely not! You are living under my rules, son!" Tempers flare, and the situation heads toward an explosion.

If you use paraphrasing during your notebook meeting, the conversation might develop like this instead: "So, son, what you are saying is that you think your current bedtime is unreasonable, and you would like a different bedtime. Did I hear you correctly?" Your son acknowledges that you paraphrased his words correctly, and you simply write down his words on the notebook-meeting agenda. Your son will most likely enjoy the fact that you acknowledged his wish and wrote it down. What a powerful affirmation for your son!

When David explains this example in his seminars, he is very quick to say, "Now, this does not mean that you *agree* with your son or that you are *agreeing* to the 11:00 p.m. request." Later in the notebook meeting, you will have a chance to explain that, as the parent, you might be willing to consider a later bedtime, but also, as the parent, you have the final say. Do you see how paraphrasing can be empowering and bring clarity at the same time? The truth is that we would all communicate better if we chose to use paraphrasing during any conversation. Please commit to it!

When you use paraphrasing with your spouse or partner, it also does not mean that you agree with what is being said, but it does communicate the message that you are *listening*. This is so powerful! When you see the transformation that happens when someone finally believes he or she has been heard, this will help both or all of you take a step closer to working *together.*

Along with paraphrasing, please explain the rule that interruptions are not allowed. If arguing is the usual way of communicating in your family, this rule will be so important to having a successful notebook meeting. You could use a prop for the person who is speaking to hold as a reminder. It could be a tennis ball, a special toy, or even a whisk from the kitchen as a pretend microphone. A little good-hearted humor always helps. The rule is that no one except the person holding the prop can speak. The prop then gets passed around the group to allow each person a time to speak without interruptions.

With some good strategies for communicating and thorough preparation before the meeting, I believe you are ready to begin! *You are ready to start recording your first notebook meeting.*

WHAT IN THE WORLD DO YOU SAY?

As I wrote in chapter five, *tell your truths.*

> "Hey, honey, I know lately we've been super busy, and things seem to be spiraling out of control. Our lives are very stressful, and we have been arguing more than usual. I don't want us to keep living like this, and I know you don't want it this way, either. The reason I wanted to meet with you today is because I have a solution that will help us. It's called the notebook meeting. It's a process of meeting with each other and developing plans to solve problems and accomplish our dreams. I have been reading all about the process, and I want your help. It starts with us making a list of problem areas that are in the way of us living the lives we really want. Instead of yelling at each other about our problem areas, I hope we can agree to help each other fix what is in the way of a better life for us. Every time we meet to have a notebook meeting, we'll write everything down in our notebook that I have here. The first step is to write our notebook-meeting agenda. We start by listing the things that are not working for us right now. Let me share what I have written, and then I can write your thoughts. Our notebook meetings will be

productive if we follow some communication guidelines I learned in the book. Let me list them for you."

"Hey, kids, I know that you don't think you have much say in what happens in our family. I remember last week when you guys said that Dad and I don't understand you or trust you to do anything. Dad and I want you to know that you do have a say and that we do trust you. The reason we are meeting today is because I have a solution that will help us talk about this and manage everything better. It's called the notebook meeting. It's a process of meeting with one another and developing plans to solve problems and work on the dreams we have. I have been reading all about the process, and I want your help. It starts with us making a list of problem areas that are in the way of us living the lives we really want. Instead of yelling at one another about our problem areas, I hope we can agree to help one another fix what is in the way of better lives for us. Our notebook meetings will be productive if we follow some communication guidelines I learned in the book. Let me list them for you."

"Sweetie, I know that for years we have dreamed of opening our own shop. I discovered something that will help us make that happen. It's called the notebook meeting. It is a process of meeting with one another and developing plans to accomplish our dreams. I've been reading all about the process, and I want your help. It starts with us making a list of problem areas that are in the way of us living the lives we really want. Together, I believe we can create a plan that will finally get us on the path to better lives. Our notebook meetings will be productive if we follow some communication guidelines I learned in the book. Let me list them for you."

Come back to these words every time you need to! You are absolutely ready to continue your meeting as you follow the agenda below.

THE FIRST NOTEBOOK-MEETING AGENDA

Here is a sample blank template for your first notebook-meeting agenda. The agenda you create can have any number of items and lines. This is a format guide.

I. Journal the specifics:

_____

_____

_____

_____

_____

_____

_____

THE FIRST NOTEBOOK MEETING

II. Agenda items:

1. _____

2. _____

3. _____

4. _____

III. The whys:

1. _____

2. _____

3. _____

4. _____

IV. Action plans and dates of completion:

1. _____

2. _____

3. _____

4. _____

THE NOTEBOOK-MEETING AGENDA *EXAMPLE*

Now let me elaborate and give you the specifics of what you could write:

I. Journal the specifics.

Here you will record the date, your intentions, and information about where you are for this meeting. If you are single and conducting the notebook meetings with yourself, please do not skip this part! Take the time to write your thoughts and feelings, and describe the moment. Are you sitting in a coffee shop, enjoying a favorite treat? Are you in the bathtub, with candles lit? Yes, the pages may get splashed a little, but what a great place to make important life decisions! Your journaling here can be simple or elaborate. No need to worry about perfect grammar. Once, when David and I met in a state park near a lake, I drew feathers in the margin next to the journaling section to remind me of the ducks that swam by. *Make your journaling meaningful.* Do your best to describe the event. Whether you are single or not, your notebook will become a treasure. (I wish you could know this now. You will so enjoy rereading your notebook meetings.) When David and I meet, this is our favorite part to write. We take turns writing each time we meet. Here are some excerpts from the journaling part of our notebook meetings.

July 21, 2007

Chattooga River—We hiked from Sandy Ford on the Bartram Trail. David and I are on an overnight trip. We needed to reconnect and have some away time. It's been a busy summer. We rebuilt our deck together. It's beautiful, but it was a huge challenge...We are meeting to decide how to focus our time before the school year starts.

June 24, 2009
We're in the car, headed back home after our long trip to Virginia,
Pennsylvania, Maryland, DC, and back to Virginia. Pete and
Patricia's wedding was wonderful. We are glad we were able to be
there. We loved going through Annapolis. David had an awesome
softshell crab sandwich; Stuart enjoyed a delicious crab and shrimp
salad. In DC we had so much fun walking to see the sights...We are
meeting to discuss ways to improve our communication and ways to
revive our spirits during busy times of the year.

Your writing might sound like this:

I. Journal the specifics:

September 24, 2016—We [list names] are all sitting around the table
for our first notebook meeting. It's a cool fall morning, and we just
had banana-nut pancakes. We are meeting together to plan ways
we can function better as a family. We agree we have been too busy
lately, and we haven't enjoyed time together as a family. We want to
improve our home life.

II. Agenda items:

In this section you will begin listing the clutter and chaos. You
have to start where you are. You have to start with what is blocking
your family from living your best life. The good news is that you have
already done the hard work of listing these things. **The Assessment
#1: My List of the Obvious** and **Assessment #2: Digging Deeper**
work sheets you completed from chapter three have the information for you! Sharing this information successfully with your family,
without blame and judgment, is your challenge here. Before you start

writing this section, explain what this means to your family. Tell your truths again.

"There are things that happen in our family that are keeping us from being happy right now. I want to get your thoughts about them. I think we can talk about them and make plans to change things for the better. Let me tell you some things I have been thinking about, and then you can share your thoughts."

This is where you list some of the items from your life assessments. Sometimes listing it all is overwhelming. Before this meeting, review **Assessment #1: My List of the Obvious** from chapter three.

You might start by saying and writing something like this:

II. Agenda items:
- Our evenings are too hectic. No sit-down dinners as a family.
- Sometimes we use disrespectful language to talk with one another.
- Our garage is a mess; we can't find things; it looks horrible.

Then you can say this:

"These are some things I think we can work on and fix to make our daily lives better. Does anyone else have something to add? Please just tell me the things you want to talk about during our meeting. I will list them here, and then we will all work together to find solutions. Our notebook meetings will help us fix the problems without resorting to conflict or screaming as we usually do."

Your son might say, and you will write:

It's hard to do my homework, because we have one computer. (Jack)

Your husband might say:

The cable bill has been too high lately. Someone keeps ordering movies. (Dad)

Your daughter might say:

I hate when you and Dad argue. (Chloe)

While you are attempting to write down the agenda items, others may begin to do more than just list. They may want to complain and blame. As the parent, or simply as the notebook-meeting manager, remind all involved that you wanted to meet to *solve* problems and to make things better.

This can really be a danger zone. This is the spot where major breakdowns could happen in the middle of your notebook meeting if this part is not handled with care. Why is this a danger zone? Well, before you can brainstorm solutions to the items you have on your agenda, you have to look at them. You have to take a real, honest look at why the problems are happening. This is where feelings could be hurt, and you could meet resistance if this part is not handled with care.

If you see a family member begin to head toward the danger zone of using judgmental, angry, or hurtful words, then this is a good time to remind everyone of your communication guidelines. Do some paraphrasing on the spot! Your modeling of the paraphrasing strategy can really minimize tension as others see you just sticking to the facts with no judgment or blame.

Let me explain what I mean. Perhaps one item on the agenda is that "the garage is too messy." What if the garage is too messy because your gardening tools are all over the place? What if it is because your son and husband are rebuilding a car? What if it is too messy because your daughter moved back home, and her boxes are filling your space? These are all normal reasons that anyone's garage becomes a nightmare. Now that you are having a notebook meeting, you are going to find a solution to the problem. No need to argue or complain about it anymore!

III. The whys

As I explained before, your tone and approach to handling all matters will help your meeting move forward in ways that are constructive for all, not destructive. Here is the next step that will keep you moving forward. It is another strategy that will bring clarity. On the template for each agenda item, I want you to ask your team to help fill in **the whys.** (See examples ahead.) Ask them to help you do this by using nonjudgmental, honest statements.

It can sound like this:

"OK, now that we have a great agenda, help me to write **the whys** for each item. I am not asking for complaints or accusations right now. I want your sincere help in working toward finding solutions to our problems instead of allowing them to negatively affect our family. This will lead us right to our action plans. So for the garage problem, do you all agree it is because my gardening tools are spread out, Dad and Jack are rebuilding the car, and Chloe's boxes are in the space where I normally park my car? Great. Now that we understand **the whys,** we can brainstorm concrete plans to make the garage situation better."

For each item on your agenda, what you write might look like this:

III. The whys (the numbers on this list correspond to the numbers on the agenda):

1. *Kids' sports practice during the week*
2. *We're not taking time to listen and communicate well, because we are so busy.*
3. *Gardening tools, car project, Chloe's boxes*
4. *Both kids using computer at the same time*
5. *During Jack's sleepover party, he and his friends ordered and watched three movies.*
6. *Dad and I have not spent time together because of our hectic life, and we're frustrated.*

Discussing **the whys** for the items on your agenda can help bring clarity for all. **The whys** get to the true nature of each problem. For example, perhaps one item on your agenda is that your daughter always leaves her beauty products all over the counter in the bathroom. The why? Some may think she is not being respectful of the space and others by clearing her beauty products away. Her truth? Her cans of mousse, gel, and hairspray are too tall for the drawer. She thinks leaving them on the counter is the best solution. With this information, you can now create an action plan to help her. She does not need a job chart to remind her; she needs a basket for her products! Yes, simple, but very, very important. The notebook meetings can bring great clarity and reduce unnecessary judgment, accusations, and frustrations.

So for each item on your agenda, take the time to really investigate the nature of the problem. Remember, as the notebook-meeting manager, you get to make the decision to say, "OK we have a great list already. Let's stop here to make plans for solving these problems."

Remember, you cannot unpack it *all* and fix it *all* in one meeting. That is why the notebook-meeting process is ongoing.

IV. Action Plans and dates for completion
This is where you plan the good work!
This is where things happen!

WHAT IS AN ACTION PLAN?

Action plans are the plans you (or all of you) create to solve problems or manage an agenda item. Ask everyone for their suggestions on what to do, and *decide as a team* which plan to choose. Let everyone talk about the specific actions the problem needs, and then assign responsibilities for completing the actions to the appropriate person or to one who volunteers. The next step is to decide together the date the action can be completed. Setting a **date for completion** is an important part of accountability.

If you are stumped about how to actually create an action plan to solve an issue, then perhaps the action plan you write is to research solutions. You can agree to research the problem together, and then decide in the next notebook meeting what steps will work the best for you. Ideas and step-by-step instructions for almost anything, whether it is organizing your pantry, creating a budget, managing your time, asking for a raise, starting a business, or building a storage cabinet are right at your fingertips, just by doing an online search.

Creating an **action plan** is how you decide to go forward to change things for the better. You will revisit **action plans** at the beginning of each notebook meeting and celebrate because *you will have evidence of great change, and you will be headed toward your mountaintop moments.*

As you begin to create **action plans**, you might say something like this:

"For my gardening tools, I can hang some hooks and get a storage bin so that everything will fit in the corner. What will work for you guys? A small worktable, maybe? Chloe, can we store some of your things in a different place, maybe create some "under-all-beds" storage? OK, let each of us set a date to accomplish each of these things. I will get my hooks and storage bin by next Saturday. Chloe, would you like to go with me to get some storage bins and risers for the beds? What about you guys?"

Continue in this way for each item on your agenda. This is what your notebook could look like at this point in the meeting:

I. Journal the specifics:

September 24, 2016—Mom, Dad, Chloe, and Jack are all sitting around the table for our first notebook meeting. It's a cool fall morning, and we just had banana-nut pancakes. We are meeting together to plan ways we can function better as a family. We agree we have been too busy lately, and we haven't enjoyed time together as a family. We want to improve our home life.

II. Agenda items:

1. *Our evenings are too hectic. No sit-down dinners as a family.*
2. *Sometimes we use disrespectful language to talk with one another.*
3. *Our garage is a mess; we can't find things; it looks horrible.*

4. *It's hard to do my homework because we have one computer. (Jack)*

5. *The cable bill has been too high lately. Someone keeps ordering movies. (Dad)*

6. *I hate when you and dad argue. (Chloe)*

III. The whys:

1. *Kids' sports practice during the week.*

2. *We're not taking time to listen and communicate well because we are so busy.*

3. *Gardening tools, car project, Chloe's boxes*

4. *Both kids using computer at same time*

5. *During Jack's sleepover party, he and his friends ordered and watched three movies.*

6. *Dad and I have not spent time together because of our hectic life, and we're frustrated.*

IV. Action Plans:

1. *Until sports season is over, we will have to keep eating quick meals or meals at the ballpark, but we commit to Saturday morning breakfasts and Sunday night dinners together. Dad and Jack will make Saturday breakfasts; mom and Chloe will make Sunday dinners.*
   Date of Completion: All Saturdays and Sundays until sports season is over.

2. *We agree to make our Saturday breakfasts and Sunday dinners as "family talk time," so everyone can share whatever needs sharing, the positive and the frustrations. We will record items for our next notebook meeting's agenda.*

Date of completion: All Saturdays and Sundays until sports season is over.

3. *Organize gardening tools on hooks, car parts on a worktable, and store boxes under beds.*
   Date of completion: Mom and Chloe will get hooks and bed risers by the 8th. Dad and Jack will make a table this weekend.
4. *Jack will use the computer between 8:00 and 9:00 p.m. Chloe will use the computer between 9:00 and 10:00 p.m.*
   Date of completion: times indicated.
5. *Jack will ask permission before ordering movies. He agrees to pay half the cost of movies he orders with his friends.*
   Date of completion: when friends are over.
6. *Mom and Dad agree to schedule their own private talk time on Sunday nights to catch up with each other. We commit to speaking to each other with respect.*
   Date of completion: every Sunday night.

Are you thinking, "There is no way my family could work together like that on all of those agenda items"? Is that your family's truth? It's time to change. I believe you can help. I believe you want better for your family. I believe everyone else wants better, too. Remind them of all of this. Tell them you are committed to doing the work. I know you are. It is time for better.

Keep doing the work.
Good will happen.

What now?

You are at the end of your first notebook meeting! *Smile, celebrate, discuss more, listen more, think about the possibilities,* and then...

*Schedule your next notebook meeting
while everyone is there!*

Write it down in your notebook!

EXCERPT FROM DAVID AND STUART'S NOTEBOOK MEETING:

Note: When David and I started our notebook meetings, we did not have the framework I am presenting in this book. Our notebook-meeting process has essentially been in the development phase since the beginning, but now it is ready for you! Our notebook meetings for the last twelve years represent a powerful journey of growing and working together to create a life we love living. The framework I am describing for you in this book is a recreation of over twelve years of finding our way. You do not have to find your way for twelve years. The notebook-meeting process is ready for you now. As you read the following, please know it will not match the format I want you to use. Just consider the following a "rough draft." Actually, as I reread our notebook meetings, I do not really consider them to be rough at all. Our meetings are very powerful. We know they can be powerful for you, too.

I. Journal the specifics:

October 17, 2010—David and I are traveling back home after a glorious, glorious weekend in Hilton Head to celebrate our fifth wedding anniversary. The weather was perfect. We enjoyed having free time, with no schedule to answer, lots of good seafood, and most importantly, uninterrupted time to focus on each other and our marriage. Thank you, Lord. We are discussing becoming more intentional and more focused on accomplishing business goals. David will adjust his session times and dedicate specific times for developing his seminars and retreats.

II. Agenda Items:

- Ongoing from previous meeting, items still needing our attention:
- Stuart going to graduate school
- Completing our wills
- Updating beneficiary designations
- Getting LLC
- Call Chris, the builder
- Clean office
- Make dental appts.
- Finish decorating office
- Get bulb for projector
- Stuart work on book
- Tag CDs for website
- Dating more
- More notebook meetings
- Clean house, windows (spring cleaning in fall)
- Buy business software
- Make calls about Disney trip

III. The whys:

- Discussion about Stuart going to school: Benefits: salary increase and retirement increase, increased training, professionalism, a dream fulfilled; Costs: tuition, time, energy, stress

IV. Action plans:

- David commits to conducting his sessions on Tuesday, Thursday, and Saturday mornings.
- David commits to completing his paperwork by Sunday at 9:00 p.m. If he doesn't complete his paperwork by Sunday night, he will complete it by Monday afternoon.
- Stuart will print a work calendar to show this.
- We will reevaluate in two weeks.
- Stuart will research this week to find two top graduate school choices.
- Will and beneficiaries: We need to look at what we currently have (put it down on paper) and reorganize if needed. David and Stuart will work on this together.

CHAPTER SEVEN

CONTINUING THE PROCESS

You are just getting started.
Don't stop now!

Going Forward

The first one is done. *You had a notebook meeting!* It's all recorded in your notebook.

So what now?

Well, you will continue having notebook meetings, but there is a little more work to do to make your meetings even more...*powerful.*

FOLLOWING THROUGH ON ACTION PLANS

After every meeting it is important, of course, that everyone follows through on the action plans, especially *you*. You are the leader in this process for now until everyone understands the power and sees the possibilities. So, go forward with encouraging reminders and offers of help *only*—no nagging allowed. Absolutely no nagging allowed. If someone does not meet the action-plan deadline, you can discuss this at the next meeting, and everyone will help solve the problem. *Unfinished action plans are simply continued on the next notebook-meeting agenda.*

There are many legitimate reasons that you or others may not complete action plans. Continuing the example from earlier, perhaps Dad and Jack did not finish making the worktable for the garage. They purchased the materials, cut the wood, and started construction, but the project took more time than estimated. All that is needed is to review that agenda item and set a new deadline. No fussing, yelling, or shaming needed. Just keep looking forward. Yes, it really can work that way.

Every time David and I have a notebook meeting, we start by reviewing the action plans from the previous meeting. There are plenty of instances where we checked off many plans as completed, and there are many times when we did not. When we do not complete an action plan, we simply discuss why the plan was not completed and then create a new deadline or change the steps in the action plan as needed.

Remember, the notebook-meeting process is different from anything you have tried before. This is an opportunity for you or you and your family to work in new ways to find a higher, better path for going forward. If you have struggled with lack of confidence or experienced repeated failures in making progress or working together as a team, know that this time *it will be different.* Grab onto hope and possibility, and do not let go. Maintain an encouraging outlook. Allow grace and forgiveness to be a part of the process whenever needed. Be an example of this for everyone included. Speak the words that demonstrate all of this:

"Thanks for trying. We'll keep working on it."

"How can I help?"

"It's OK. Let's add it to the next agenda."

"Maybe we all need to rethink this."

As I said before, No fussing, yelling, or shaming needed. Just keep looking forward. Yes, it really can work that way.

CREATING THE NEXT AGENDA

Creating the agenda for the next meeting is similar to creating the agenda for the first meeting, except that now you will have suggestions and items from others. Even if the next notebook meeting is scheduled for two weeks away, explain to everyone that they can start thinking now of other matters that they would like to include on the agenda for the next notebook meeting. Tell them to keep their own lists of items to discuss, and you will add them to the next agenda when you meet. At the beginning of each notebook meeting, you will ask for and write down everyone's agenda items.

Over time you may decide that you want a different method of compiling agenda items in preparation for your next notebook meeting. You may decide to leave the notebook out and let others add to a list. If you are a crafter, you could create a beautiful notebook-meeting agenda chalkboard to hang in the kitchen. Be creative, and make a system that will work for everyone.

Remember also to look back to the assessments you completed in chapter three as you work to create the agenda for the next notebook meeting. You can keep pulling items from the assessments. In fact, for your first few notebook meetings, you will continue including the items that you originally listed on the assessments, the items that represent your current chaos and clutter. You must do the work to address each item you wrote on **Assessment #1: My List of the Obvious** and **Assessment #2: Digging Deeper.** If you do not take action on the items you wrote on your first assessment, they will continue to steal the energy you need to work toward your mountaintop moments.

With each new month you will discover that new events will happen in your life that will require your attention in a notebook meeting. For the events that you already know are coming, such as birthdays or holidays, remember to complete **Assessment #3: Rising Higher** and **Assessment #4: Grab the Future.**

CONTINUING THE NOTEBOOK MEETING PROCESS

Now you have an overall understanding of how the notebook-meeting process works. You will continue to have notebook meetings, work on action plans, organize your life, and clear the clutter and chaos that is currently in the way of your mountaintop moments. Yes, this is the process, except there is one exciting additional detail you need to know and implement: *It is time to celebrate!*

CELEBRATE THE WORK

For the second and all consecutive notebook meetings, there is an important part of the actual meeting that is different from the first notebook meeting:

You get to start with a celebration!

For every notebook meeting after the first one, you will start by looking back at the notes of the previous meeting, reading the action plans aloud, *and checking off the items as completed!* Please do not miss the power of this new part of the process I just added. *Start each meeting hereafter with a celebration!* Take time at the beginning of each notebook meeting to celebrate everyone's success and hard work! These moments are so important. They help everyone see the possibilities. The celebrations help everyone see the power of working as a team to solve problems.

If you or someone did not complete an action plan, you will just carry that item forward. Discuss and analyze, without judgment or shame, why the action plan was not completed. There may be a very practical, legitimate reason.

THE NOTEBOOK-MEETING AGENDA

Here is a sample blank template for all the rest of your notebook-meeting agendas. You can have any number of items and lines. This is just a format guide.

I. Journal the specifics:

_____

_____

_____

_____

_____

II. Items completed from last agenda: *(Celebrate!)*

_____

_____

_____

_____

III. Agenda items *(include items to carry over from last meeting):*

1. _____

2. _____

3. _____

4. _____

IV. The whys:

1. _____

2. _____

3. _____

4. _____

V. Action plans and dates of completion:

1. _____

2. _____

3. _____

4. _____

EXCERPT FROM DAVID AND STUART'S NOTEBOOK MEETING:

I. Journal the specifics:

We're at Johnny Carino's for dinner. It's the night before our school year starts. We're starting a tradition of celebrating the end of summer and looking forward to a new school year.

II. Items completed from last agenda:

I'm looking at our list from the last meeting; we've improved at maximizing our time together and minimizing our household tasks. We've continued working on our finances; we hope to close on the refinancing this week.

III. Agenda items *(include items to carry over from last meeting):*

1. *Continue to work on website.*
2. *Continue home improvement projects: redecorating bedroom, landscaping, painting kitchen, get carpet cleaned.*
3. *Move Liz to Valdosta.*
4. *We're having trouble cooking meals during the week.*

IV. The whys *(no need to discuss items 1–3 from previous meeting):*
1. *Working out (Stuart runs; David in gym) is a priority for both of us. There isn't enough time after work to do this and cook a good meal.*

V. Action plans and dates of completion:
1. *David will meet with JHouse Media to discuss final changes to the website. First, we'll review the contract by next Saturday.*
2. *Stuart will focus on finishing the bedroom by next Sunday, if not sooner. She just needs to shop for the comforter set.*
3. *Move Liz to Valdosta on Saturday. Everything's ready!*
4. *Stuart will look for easy crockpot recipes to help with meals during the week. We'll also make a list of meals we can cook on Sundays and freeze for later.*

THE HARD WORK

When I started to write this chapter, I *thought* I wanted to tell you the hard work was over after you had your first meeting. I *thought* I wanted to tell you that the only major challenges you will have in this process were the assessments you did to create the first agenda. I *thought* I wanted to tell you the notebook meetings will get easier, and you will breeze through the process now. But that is not really what I want to say. The truth is I do not really want the process to be easier for you.

I want the notebook-meeting process
to always be powerful for you.

Easy is not the goal. *Easy* is just not a relevant word here. **Powerful, impactful, life changing**—these words are relevant here. Your first notebook meeting gives you only a glimpse of the possibilities. Start considering how far you can go with the notebook-meeting process. You *can* get there!

> *You must keep doing the work.*
> *Good will happen.*

GRABBING THE FUTURE

Now it is time to look back at a step I said was optional in chapter three. Perhaps you included it already, but if not, we must go back and look at it. In chapter three, you completed **Assessments #1** and **#2** to identify the clutter and chaos that is keeping you from reaching your mountaintop moments. Using **Assessments #1** and **#2** is the foundation for creating your agenda for starting the notebook-meeting process, *and you are doing that work!* Keep including the items from those assessments on your agendas, and keep making action plans to get those areas of your life under control, cleared out, and no longer an issue. Remember, you are clearing the areas of your life that are taking time and energy that you could be using to reach your mountaintop moments.

In chapter three, I actually asked you to give yourself four months to work on the items from the **Assessments #1 and #2** and then go back and complete **Assessments #3 and #4.** You do not have to wait four months. If you are ready to move forward with living the true *proactive life*, keep reading and get started!

Note: What you are about to read is exactly what I wrote in chapter three about **Assessment #3 and Assessment #4**. I simply copied and pasted it here for your convenience.

Assessment #3: Rising Higher
Assessment #4: Grab the Future

It is time for two more assessments. These two assessments will lead you to add new items to your agendas for subsequent notebook meetings. Each assessment has a purpose. First, you get to start dreaming a little. Remember the mountaintop moments I talked about in chapter one? Those dreams you have not touched in a while? Well, they are about to become a little more solid. You are about to work them into your life. Here is how the dreaming works: stand on your tippy toes, and look over the foothills (the laundry, debt, negative relationships) in your way. Set your eyes on the other side of the foothills, and then look to the mountaintops beyond. Gaze at the future, and imagine yourself there. When your foothills of clutter and chaos are gone, where do you want to direct your energy?

What are your mountaintop moments?
What are your dreams?

Have you always wanted to go back to school? Are you interested in a different career? Do you want to start your own business? Do you want to publish a book? What home-improvement projects are on your wish list? When your vision includes your family, what are those mountaintop moments? Do you see a family that no longer yells at one another? Do you see the family that works together to complete the household chores? Or maybe your vision hits a little closer to your heart: Are you seeing a family that *wants* to spend time with one another? Is there a dream vacation you really want to make happen? The dreams and the possibilities are endless. There are many mountaintops waiting for you.

Sometimes it is best to choose only a few dreams to come into focus before you get overwhelmed. Later, after working through some notebook meetings and reaching a few mountaintops, *you can choose more*. It will always be up to you.

Secondly, you will look to the future and record which upcoming events will need your attention. Looking ahead and making plans for future events is being *proactive*. This is where you start directing your life instead of letting life direct you. Yes, it is time for two more work sheets. On the **Assessment #3: Rising Higher** work sheet, you will list your mountaintop moments, and on **Assessment #4: Grab the Future**, you will list events in the immediate future that will need your attention. It is time to give it a try!

Here is more good news: just as I told you when you started the other assessments, these, too, will become second nature to you after you start the notebook meetings. You will not have to come back to these work sheets every time you have a meeting, unless you want. The work sheets are designed to help you learn the notebook-meeting process. These are your starting points. You are using them for practice.

On the next page you will find the sample **Assessment #3: Rising Higher** and **Assessment #4: Grab the Future** work sheets. On the pages that follow the sample, you will find a blank one for you to use.

Assessment #3: Rising Higher: (Sample)

1. WHAT ARE MY MOUNTAINTOP MOMENTS?	2. WHAT DO I NEED TO GET THERE?
Home Having a craft room	Redo the guest bedroom
Family Having Sunday dinners with all of my family	Talk to my sister-in-law, plan it
Health Change my lifestyle to consistently get more sleep	I don't know yet.
Work Submit my project proposal	Make an appointment with my boss.
Social Life Join a hiking group	Call the park to get info, or search online.
Spiritual Life Join a bible study group	Ask at church

Assessment #4: Grab the Future: (Sample)

1. LIST UPCOMING EVENTS:	2. WHAT DO YOU NEED TO HANDLE IT?
Birthdays Husband's	Arrange family celebration, purchase gift
Family Dentist appts for children Plan vacation	Let everyone know, check calendar Save $, decide on trip specifics
Home/Car Need oil change	Schedule this
Social Tailgating Party	Decide menu, make list of supplies

CONTINUING THE PROCESS

Now it's your turn! Use this blank one, or recreate your own in your notebook.

Assessment #3: Rising Higher

1. WHAT ARE MY MOUNTAINTOP MOMENTS?	2. WHAT DO I NEED TO GET THERE?
Home	
Family	
Health	
Work	
Social Life	
Spiritual Life	

Assessment #4: Grab the Future

1. LIST UPCOMING EVENTS:	2. WHAT DO YOU NEED TO HANDLE IT?

Like the work you did on **Assessments #1** and **#2**, the work you do on these sheets will also be items on your notebook-meeting agendas, but you will handle them differently. When you discuss these items during a notebook meeting, you can directly go to creating action plans for them. The action plans will be more obvious for these items.

This is what the proactive life is all about!

When you start living the proactive life with the notebook meetings, you will be doing two things: choosing which mountaintop moment you would like to reach first, and planning for whatever events are coming (birthdays, holidays, work deadlines, school happenings). You will start taking charge of day-to-day life. You will no longer live a life of reacting to whatever is happening at the moment. This is what I hope for you.

A DIFFERENT LIFE: MAKING THE SHIFT

As you continue to have notebook meetings, you and everyone who participates will make a gradual life shift from no longer living the old, chaotic, *reactive life* to experiencing the joy, peace, and strength of the *proactive life. You* will be the ones in charge of your days. Unanticipated events will no longer control you or derail your day and consume your time and energy. *You* will determine how the events of your day will go. *You* will make plans that allow you to be more productive, creative, and efficient. Your home will become a peaceful sanctuary that provides security, love, and growth. Your relationships will be filled with intention, desire, and deeper connection. The clutter and chaos of the past, both the physical and the emotional, will go away.

As you have more and more notebook meetings, the power of the successes multiplies and spills over into other parts of your life. It is one of the dynamics of the notebook meetings that I cannot really explain for you. You will have to live it to understand it. Just for a moment, try to imagine the possibilities: you become more organized at work, and others begin to see you as a visionary because of your forward thinking, and your child's progress at school improves because he or she learns what it means to have a successful work ethic and sees the strength of the family growing.

Trust the process.
You will reach a higher path.

As you begin to see success in the process, you will realize you are living in a different place. You will realize you are experiencing a different type of existence. Life will make sense. Life will be better.

You and all who participate will know that good can and will happen for your family when you work together. Confidence will grow. Hope will abound.

So, now let's review the entire notebook-meeting process:

Components of a Notebook Meeting:

_____ You have a date, time, menu, and location.

_____ You have a notebook and a pen.

_____ A printed calendar is helpful for planning. If it is printed, everyone can see it.

_____ If you are preparing food or a meal, have it ready before the meeting begins.

_____ Others have agenda items to add to the list.

Agenda items include current clutter and chaos, and future items, *including mountaintop moments!*

_____ You have a template for the entire notebook meeting:

_____ Journal the specifics of the meeting.

_____ Review and check off the previous action plans.

_____ Write any incomplete agenda items.

_____ Celebrate!

_____ Write the new agenda items.

_____ Write the "whys."

_____ Develop new action plans with dates for completion.

_____ Decide on the next notebook meeting date.

In time, this all will become automatic for you. You will learn to make it your own. You will learn to record the meetings in a way that makes sense to you. As you know, David and I have been living with the notebook meetings now for about twelve years. Our mind-sets about our daily lives are automatically in "notebook-meeting format." When something comes up, we analyze it and create action plans in our heads. Our mindset is *proactive*. We speak in "action-plan" terms. We thrive on teamwork. We celebrate our accomplishments. Our lives make sense. We want your life to make sense, too.

This is where we all need to live
to be our best for the greater good.

CHAPTER EIGHT

IT'S YOUR TURN

Make it your own.

You've got this.

It is time to let you go. *You* have completed a lot of hard work that needed to be done. *You* decided it was time to clear out the stuff. *You* committed to a different life, and *you* are on your way. Right now it does not really matter if your family joined you for the ride or not. What matters is that *you* started.

In the Introduction of this book, I wrote a list of guiding principles. Let me review and elaborate on these principles. Now that you have read the book, you will understand these additional thoughts.

GUIDING PRINCIPLES OF
THE NOTEBOOK MEETING PROCESS

1. **You *will* organize your life. This time it will stick.** Now that you know the process, you know that you can add anything to your agenda, and develop an action plan to manage it. *Anything.*

If a previous agenda item becomes a problem again, you know what to do. Put it on the agenda again. Discuss it again. Develop an action plan for it again. Check it off again. Done. No shaming, no judgment; just plenty of grace.

2. **You *will* accomplish goals that have previously seemed unreachable.** You will no longer be permanently distracted from the path that takes you to your mountaintop moments. Yes, we all get distracted momentarily, but now there is no reason to stay stuck. You *will* clear the clutter and chaos from your life and direct your energy to accomplishing your goals. Your dreams *will* become your reality. You *will* know how to work for them, and you *will* experience success. Yes, you *will.*

3. **It is an ongoing process. You will never want it to end.** The power of the notebook meetings comes from the fact that it is a process that *you* direct. The notebook-meeting process will become a part of your life because it matters. The work you do will change your mind-set, your outlook, and your confidence. The notebook meetings will change your life.

4. **You are not perfect, and neither am I. We can forgive ourselves for all the times we did not get it right. This time we *will.*** Allow yourself to be imperfect as you work through life. Give yourself room to make mistakes. The notebook meetings give you a chance to start over and do better every day. The choice is always up to you.

5. **No one else can do the work for you. You have to do the work. You *will* be able to figure it out.** Here is the good news: you are ready! You now have a vision for how *to work to change your life.* You are capable, and you will see results. Our human existence does not allow us to have peace if we are stuck. It is only when we are growing and serving that our soul experiences what it means to live a full life. Do not miss this. Do the work.

Every time you choose to have a notebook meeting, you are choosing a higher path for yourself that will affect others. When you start the notebook meetings, you will bring order, purpose, meaning, intention, and growth back into your life. All of that goodness will affect the world.

Our world needs order, purpose, meaning,
intention, and growth. It is time to get started.

I BELIEVE

PART ONE

I believe we all want better.

I believe that what helps us put one foot in front of the other every single day is the hope that we can do better.

I believe the more we all want to be living for the higher good for everyone, the better we believe our souls are capable.

We want the peace of knowing our lives matter for the higher good.

Whether it is affecting the life of one person or a million people on this earth, we want to be a part of that change.

We want to do the good.
We want to be the good.

I believe we all want better for ourselves, our others, our families, our friends, our schools, our churches, our colleagues, our homeless, our elderly, our helpless, our hopeless, our lost, our found, our nation, and our world.

I believe we want better for the world because we realize we are connected. The good energy I create spills over into your life. The good energy you create spills over into my life.

It is part of God's plan for us all.

I believe we want to keep God's good energy cycle going.

I believe when we mess up, we can try again. This is God's grace, another way He loves us. I believe you can know this, too. When you understand grace, you will know there are endless possibilities. We all live for the possibilities.

PART TWO

I also believe some of you think you aren't capable of changing the world.

I believe I know why.

It has to do with the damage. You believe your souls are irreparably broken, and you are *less than*.

You believe the hurtful chapters in your life have chipped away at your soul so that what is left can take you only so far. "My broken soul can't help someone else," you say.

I believe our souls are always *whole. They are not broken, and there are no chips nor pieces missing.*

I do believe parts of our souls are covered up *for now.* Yes, we have darkness. The darkness is like a layer of black paint that has been applied in large and small swatches to cover the light we all are.

Our souls have been shining inside us all our lives. Our souls have not gone anywhere. Our souls have not been taken away piece by piece. They have simply been *covered up.*

Choose to be uncovered.

I believe our desire to live for the higher good appears when we clear the darkness.

Choose to clear the darkness.

I believe we can do better when we uncover what is hiding in us behind the darkness.

Choose to uncover your light, *God's light.*

I believe, when given the choice, we would all choose to share God's light.

Let's get started.

ACKNOWLEDGMENTS

First, thank you to David and Liz.

It is always better with a team.

Thank you, David, for knowing we needed to share our notebook meetings and for giving me the encouragement and the space to write. Thank you for every time you grabbed the pen and recorded our notebook meetings.

Thank you, Liz, for using the friendship card when we needed it. You and your girls came through with overwhelming support.

Liz, Christina, Jennifer, and Becca, your eyes saw what mine could not. Thank you for sharing your best with me. Your contributions will change lives.

Finally, *all glory to God.*